Magic Dance

Books by Thinley Norbu

A Brief Fantasy History of a Himalayan

A Cascading Waterfall of Nectar

Echoes: The Boudhanath Teachings

Gypsy Gossip and Other Advice

Magic Dance: The Display of the Self-Nature of the Five Wisdom Dakinis

The Small Golden Key to the Treasure of the Various Essential Necessities of General and Extraordinary Buddhist Dharma

The Sole Panacea: A Brief Commentary on the Seven-Line Prayer *to Guru Rinpoche That Cures the Suffering of the Sickness of Karma and Defilement*

Welcoming Flowers from across the Cleansed Threshold of Hope: An Answer to Pope John Paul II's Criticism of Buddhism

White Sail: Crossing the Waves of Ocean Mind to the Serene Continent of the Triple Gems

THINLEY NORBU

MAGIC DANCE

The Display of the Self-Nature
of the Five Wisdom Dakinis

SHAMBHALA
Boulder
1999

Shambhala Publications, Inc.
2129 13th Street
Boulder, Colorado 80302
www.shambhala.com

13   12   11   10   9   8   7

Printed in the United States of America
♾ This edition is printed on acid-free paper that meets the
American National Standards Institute z39.48 Standard.
♻ Shambhala Publications makes every effort to print on recycled
paper. For more information please visit
www.shambhala.com.
Shambhala Publications is distributed worldwide by Penguin
Random House, Inc., and its subsidiaries.

Library of Congress Cataloging-in-Publication Data
Thinley, Norbu.
    Magic dance: the display of the self-nature of the five wisdom
dakinis / Thinley Norbu.—1st Shambhala ed.
        p.   cm.
    ISBN 978-0-87773-885-5 (pbk.: alk. paper)
    1. Buddhism—Doctrines.   2. Ḍākinī (Buddhist deity)   I. Title.
BQ4160.T47   1998   98-20349
294.3'420423—dc21   CIP

I bow to my own Wisdom Mind,
which is my best wisdom teacher,
the source of all visible and invisible qualities.
Sentient beings are always in time and place.
If sentient beings are in time,
my wisdom teacher dances magically in time.
If sentient beings are in place,
my wisdom teacher dances magically in place.
If really examined, you never remain anywhere.
You are only display.
To whatever never remains,
to you, my best wisdom teacher, I bow.

Contents

Magic Dance

Dedication

T HIS BOOK is not written according to any one tradition. Countless traditions of writing based on endless ordinary dualistic conceptions, on sublime intelligent compassion, and on nondualistic wisdom pervade everywhere, so readers can choose whatever tradition they like.

Some people like to pick flowers and put them on an altar in a beautiful vase to offer to the gods. Others like to pick flowers and put them in a beautiful vase to decorate their home. Some people like to weave flowers into a garland to wear around their neck, and others like to weave them into a crown to wear on their head. Still, some people prefer not to pick flowers at all, but rather to leave them to grow naturally in an open sunlit meadow.

No matter what tradition we choose, it always comes from the five elements, returns to the five elements, and remains in the five elements. I have written this book in order to establish in a simple, natural way the basis, path, and result of tradition, which are the elements.

I began this book in my friends' samadhi shrine rooms in New York, the most crazy lively city in the world, appearing like a splendid whirling mountain. I finished this book in my friends' samadhi shrine room in Paris, the most elegant paradise city in the world, appearing like a beautiful fantasy mandala. In both these cities, my loyal friends showed me their generosity, their kindness, their integrity, and their nobility.

Buddha Shakyamuni said, "All phenomena arise from circumstances. Because good circumstances can arise through good intention, whatever we pray for will appear." So may all sentient beings, especially those who helped me with this book, learn to use the pure secret essence of the elements' energy to attain enlightenment.

MAGIC DANCE

Five Wisdom Sisters,

If we do not complement you,
You become five witches,
Making us ill and bringing us suffering.
Because we cannot banish you,
Always our fate depends on you.

Five Wisdom Sisters,

If we do complement you,
You become five angels,
Making us healthy and bringing us happiness.
Because we cannot separate from you,
Always our fate depends on you.

Five Wisdom Sisters,

Nothing can be done without depending on your mood.
Farmers cannot grow their crops,
Politicians cannot rule their countries,
Engineers cannot work their machines,
Doctors cannot heal their patients,
Scientists cannot do their research,
Philosophers cannot make their logic,
Artists cannot create their art,
Without depending on your mood.

Five Wisdom Sisters,

Nothing can be known without depending on your grace.
Tibetan lamas cannot chant with cool highland habit,
Indian gurus cannot sing with warm lowland habit,
Japanese roshis cannot sit with dark cushion habit,
Muslim sheikhs cannot dance with bright robed habit,
Christian priests cannot preach with loud-voiced habit,
Jewish rabbis cannot pray with soft-voiced habit
Without depending on your grace.

Dedication

Five Wisdom Sisters,

Even the most mysterious miracles cannot occur
without complementing your purity.
Buddha Shakyamuni cannot rest with the tranquil
gaze of his lotus eyes underneath the Bodhi tree,
Guru Padmasambhava cannot play magically with
countless sky-walking dakinis,
Lord Jesus cannot walk weightlessly across the water,
Prophet Moses cannot see the radiantly burning bush,
Brahmin Sarahapa cannot straighten arrows, singing
wisdom hymns with his arrowmaker girl,
Crazy saint Tilopa cannot eat fish and torture Naropa,
Greatest yogi Milarepa cannot remain in his cave,
singing and accepting hardships
Without complementing your purity.

You are so patient.
Whoever wants to stay,
If you don't exist,
Cannot stay.
Whoever wants to go,
If you don't exist,
Cannot go.
Whoever wants to taste or touch,
If you don't exist,
Cannot taste or touch.
Whatever our actions,
You are always supporting
Patiently without complaining.
But we ignorant beings
Are always ungrateful,
Stepping on you,
Calling you Earth.

You are so constant.
Whoever wants to be purified,

If you don't exist,
Cannot be purified.
Whoever wants to quench their thirst,
If you don't exist,
Cannot quench their thirst.
Whoever wants to hear,
If you don't exist,
Cannot hear.
Whatever our actions,
You are always flowing
Ceaselessly without complaining.
But we desiring beings
Are always ungrateful,
Splashing you,
Calling you Water.

You are so clear.
Whoever wants to fight,
If you don't exist,
cannot fight.
Whoever wants to love,
If you don't exist,
Cannot love.
Whoever wants to see,
If you don't exist,
Cannot see.
Whatever our actions,
You are always glowing
Unobscuredly without complaining.
But we proud beings
Are always ungrateful
Smothering you,
Calling you Fire.

You are so light.
Whoever wants to rise,

Dedication

If you don't exist,
Cannot rise.
Whoever wants to move,
If you don't exist,
Cannot move.
Whoever wants to smell,
If you don't exist,
Cannot smell.
Whatever our actions,
You are always moving
Weightlessly without complaining.
But we envious beings
Are always ungrateful,
Fanning you,
Calling you Air.

You are so open.
Whoever wants to exist,
If you don't exist,
Cannot exist.
Whoever doesn't want to exist,
If you don't exist,
Cannot cease to exist.
Whoever wants to know phenomena,
If you don't exist,
Cannot know phenomena.
Whatever our actions,
You are always welcoming
Spaciously without complaining.
But we ignorant beings
Are always ungrateful,
Emptying you,
Calling you Space.

You are our undemanding slave,
Tirelessly serving us,

From ordinary beings to sublime beings,
To fulfill our worldly wishes.

You are our powerful queen,
Seductively conquering us,
From ordinary beings to sublime beings,
Into desirable qualities.

You are our Wisdom Dakini,
Effortlessly guiding us with your magic dance,
From ordinary beings to sublime beings,
Into desireless qualities.

And so, I want to introduce you.

Introduction

Even if one nectar drop of your name
falls on our ears, it fills them
with the sound of Dharma for many lives.
Wondrous Triple Gems, famous for your glory,
may you always give the auspicious.

—PATRUL RINPOCHE

ALL LIMITED or limitless spheres of existence which arise, whether gross or subtle, unhappy or happy, ordinary or sublime, depend on the five elements, which are the basis of all pure and impure phenomena. Throughout samsara and nirvana, from atoms to insects, human beings and objects and machines, everything is made up of the five elements.

All generally visible measureless phenomena elements are the display of self-secret divisionless unobstructed Wisdom Mind. The nature of mirrorlike Wisdom Mind is that everything arises with infinite obstructed and unobstructed potential.

Whenever we do not recognize the pure nature of the manifestation of wisdom display, we cling to unobstructed mind's uncatchable self-arising reflection, obscuring its inseparable emptiness and luminosity, and separating the divisionless phenomena elements into subject and object. As soon as there is division, there is impurity and obstruction.

With this division, "I" becomes the subject, and what this "I" perceives becomes the object, whether one or many, lifeless or lively, inanimate or animate. With this division, there is constant moving back and forth between subject and object, which is the beginning of direction and time, between root circumstances and contributing circumstances, between rejecting and accepting unpleasant and pleasant phenomena, between bad and good intentions, and between doubting and hoping. We call this divided mind dualistic mind, which is the cause of bad and good karma.

Whenever we recognize the pure nature of the manifestation of self-secret invisible wisdom display, we are aware of the pure secret essence of the elements. With this recognition there is no subject and no object, no beginning and no end, no direction and no time, no root circumstances and no contributing circumstances, so there is no karma. With this recognition, absolute truth and relative truth become inseparable, nondualistic, clear awareness space. In this space, phenomena arise freely and this display of Wisdom Mind is not nothingness. The enlightened mind dances unobstructedly with phenomena yet has the potential to obstruct phenomena at will, like choosing to eat or not to eat.

Enlightened mind reflects all the five wisdoms in equanimity. But through ignorance, over countless lifetimes we have created conceptions and karmic habits which obscure our Wisdom Mind's lively, unobstructed, mirrorlike quality. Because of our obscured ordinary mind, our ego makes categories out of equanimity. With ego and categories come substance, with the birth of substance comes its death, and with death comes suffering. Our inert and stale karmic body and all other substances are the gross element result of our inability in previous lives to recognize the invisible secret essence of all substance. We are lost and suffering because of external staleness and internal ignorance. But even though we cannot recognize our invisible secret essence immediately, it is not necessary to think that it is far away. Our secret essence is always within the gross and subtle elements.

In general, we always believe that delusion is understood by undeluded Wisdom Mind, but really delusion is understood by ordinary deluded mind. Undeluded Wisdom Mind does not have any deluded conception because it does not have a deluded subject or object. From the relative point of view of ordinary mind, divisionless secret Wisdom Mind appears to be divided into inner and outer elements which manifest from subtle and discriminating feeling to increasingly gross and distinct form, appearing internally as flesh, blood, heat, breath, and consciousness, and externally as earth, water, fire, air, and space.

The external and internal manifestations of the outer and inner elements are linked to one another through our activities. The external substantial form of the earth element and the internal substantial form of the flesh are linked through eating. The external liquid of the water element and internal liquid of blood are linked through drinking. The external sun of the fire element and internal warmth of the body are linked through absorption. The external wind of the air element and internal wind of breath are linked through breathing. The external sky of the space element and internal sky of the mind are linked through openness. All five of the elements are interdependent and inherent within each element, enabling them to link and create the infinite display of phenomena.

Phenomena originally appear conspicuous to ordinary mind from the subtle air element out of the subtler space element. Because they are both light and invisible, they complement each other, and when the more conspicuous subtle air element is drawn to ordinary mind's subtler space element conception through karma, they engage and move together inseparably. This activity automatically generates subtle warmth, which is the essence of the subtle fire element. When the more conspicuous and substantial fire element is drawn to the subtle air element through karma, they engage and move together inseparably. This activity generates the less subtle water element. When the more conspicuous and substantial subtle water element is drawn to the subtle fire element through karma, they engage and move together inseparably. This activity generates the most conspicuous and substantial earth element.

When beings die, this process reverses direction. When the substantial form of the earth element dissolves into the water element, the body becomes pale and inert. When the moisture of the water element dissolves into the fire element, the body become dry.

When the warmth of the fire element dissolves into the air element, the body becomes cool. When the breath of the air element dissolves into the space element, mind becomes unconscious, and this is called death.

If we have the nihilist point of view and believe we are born as a result of chance or coincidence, we think that phenomena end at death or when circumstances change, so there is no basis for talk about new phenomena. If we have the eternalist point of view and believe in an invisible creator, we think that we join our creator at death, so we talk optimistically about going to heaven.

From the Buddhist point of view, it is a mistake to think like the nihilists that at the time of death the subtle elements have vanished with the gross. According to Buddhism, when the gross elements are exhausted and their powers are diminished, they dissolve into each other, becoming more and more subtle, and will again become conspicuous and reappear as inner and outer elements in the different realms of rebirth depending on karma. We continue to turn in this endless circle of birth and death until we realize, like the Lord Buddha, the lightest purest secret essence of enlightenment.

Wherever the outer and inner obstructed impure substance elements exist, the pure secret essence is inherent and pervades. Among all the gross and subtle elements, we can find both impure and pure qualities. The impure are closer to the substance appearance of the elements. The pure are closer to their substanceless source. Pure luminous yellow is the essence color of earth. Pure luminous white is the essence color of water. Pure luminous red is the essence color of fire. Pure luminous green is the essence color of air. Pure luminous blue is the essence color of space.

The substanceless source of the five manifested luminous colors is the secret substanceless wisdom energy of the five Wisdom Consorts of the five Wisdom Buddhas. Buddha-Locana is the Wisdom Consort symbolizing the earth element. Mamaki is the Wisdom Consort symbolizing the water element. Damdara-Vasini is the Wisdom Consort symbolizing the fire element. Samaya Tara is the Wisdom Consort symbolizing the air element. Dhatvisvari is the Wisdom Consort symbolizing the space element.

Introduction

Although all beings originate from the wisdom potential of the elements, the different obscured qualities are caused by the effects of karmic links. For instance, through their sense of feeling, earthworms are attracted to the earth because in previous lives they predominantly had the habit of earth's phenomena. Through their sense of touch, fish are attracted to water because in previous lives they predominantly had the habit of water's phenomena. Through their keen eyesight, vultures are attracted to light, because in previous lives they predominantly had the habit of fire's phenomena. Through their keen sense of smell dogs are attracted to air because in previous lives they predominantly had the habit of air's phenomena. Through their consciousness, some practitioners are attracted to the substanceless because in previous lives they predominantly had the habit of space's phenomena to recognize all phenomena as substanceless magic display.

If we grasp at substance with attachment, it is because with our gross element deluded minds we have created the ordinary five senses and the objects of the senses. Because we never recognize that our senses and their objects are the illusory manifestations of our obstructed gross elements, we try to reject unpleasant objects and accept pleasant objects. But because of this, positive becomes negative and there is still suffering.

Through attachment to sight, the moth is attracted to fire's beautiful light and dies from its flame. Through attachment to sound the deer pauses to hear the hunter's beautiful whistle and dies from his arrow. Through attachment to smell the male praying mantis is lured to the female and dies from her instinct to consume him. Through attachment to taste, the fish is attracted to delicious bait and dies from the fisherman's hook. Through attachment to touch the elephant is attracted to the swamp's warmth and dies in its mud.

The dominance of the karmic potentials of different elements causes the dominance of corresponding passions. For example, ordinary human beings who tended predominantly towards the earth element in previous lives have an earthy temperament connected with the passion of ignorance, whose characteristic is heaviness, solidity and immobility. Those who tended predominantly towards the water element have a fluid temperament connected with the passion of desire, whose characteristic is following-after and ever-changing. Those who tended predominantly towards the fire element have a hot temperament connected to the passion of anger, whose characteristic is burning violence, or have a simmering temperament connect to the passion of pride, whose characteristic is unreceptive one-sidedness. Those who tended predominantly towards the air element have an airy temperament connected to the passion of jealousy, whose characteristic is rejecting through clinging and grasping. Those who tended predominantly towards the space element have an unfocused temperament connected with the passion of ignorance, whose characteristic is dullness, which is basic, all-pervasive, and untouchable.

These five passions are contained within the three passions of desire, anger, and ignorance, which are the source of suffering for ordinary people. Desire creates love through attachment to pleasurable circumstances; love creates anger by controlling through grasping. The basis of both is ignorance, which creates only darkness by confusing love with anger through grasping.

> I can understand why Lord Buddha left his jeweled kingdom.
> I can understand why Lord Buddha put his brocade robes
>   aside.
> I can understand why Lord Buddha clad himself in ragged
>   cotton.
> He did this to lead ordinary beings from these three passions
>   which stem from ego, the source of all suffering.
> He did this to attain enlightenment, which is an egoless state
>   beyond suffering.

People with good karma who wish to attain enlightenment can use their subtle qualities naturally and increase their inherent purity until they no longer need to depend on gross substance and karma. By recognizing the subtle elements inherent in the gross elements, we are able to act with skillful means. For example, when people smile, their upwards-turned mouths express through the gross external elements the more subtle positive happiness within. When people glare, their wrinkled foreheads express through the gross external elements the more subtle negative anger or turbulence within. Sometimes, the subtle elements of smiling are not positive. Even though the gross element mouth is turned upwards, the subtle element behind the smile is negative, like the lure of the fisherman who tantalizes the fish with delicious bait in order to kill him. Sometimes the subtle elements of glaring are not negative. Behind some thorns, beautiful soft flowers grow. So we must be intelligent about discerning the quality of what is invisible and gain confidence about how to use negative and positive subtle elements.

What is visible to a sublime being is invisible to an ordinary person, just as what is visible to some intelligent ordinary people is invisible to shortsighted ordinary people. Intelligent people can foresee the future through deduction, while the future is totally obscure to shortsighted ordinary people. In the same way, because it is invisible to them, many people conclude that Dharma is superstition. They do not recognize that they can only penetrate the gross elements and communicate with the subtle elements by relying on the pure secret essence of the elements. Through this reliance, superior beings never exhaust their pure secret natural energy and wisdom confidence. The more they use space, which contains all the other elements inherently, the more their gross elements become subtle and light. Ultimately, when they no longer believe in finding any qualities in gross substance, they are said to be enlightened.

Good practitioners can purify their gross internal and external earth elements. When they do this, the internal earth elements of the gross nerve channels and veins become lighter and lighter, purer and purer, and as they become insubstantial, indestructible, and luminous, the distinction between the conceptions of external and internal earth elements diminishes until they have become purified into the same substanceless light essence. Padmasambhava attained this state. Because it has an indestructible vajra nature and cannot be penetrated by any circumstances, according to the Vajrayana system, this is called Vajra Wisdom Body.

Good practitioners can purify their gross internal and external air elements. When they do this, the internal air elements become lighter and lighter, purer and purer, and as they become unobstructed and clear, the distinction between the conceptions of eternal and internal air elements diminishes until they have become purified into the same enchanting sound. Some great saints in ancient times attained this state. The pure clarity of their sound was not impaired by the cracks and scratching of gross elements' vibrations and nothing could obstruct its tone, which pervades everywhere. This is called Vajra Wisdom Song.

Good practitioners can diminish the dualism of their inner subject substance mind and outer object substance phenomena. When they do this, the subtle elements become more and more vast, more and more limitless, and as they become boundless and profound, the distinction between the dualistic conception of outer and inner space elements diminishes until they have become purified into the same infinite expanse. Then everything is without beginning and without end. This is Samantabhadra, whose wisdom heart is the source of measureless and limitless knowledge, unconquered and undeceived by the illusion of dualism. This is called Vajra Wisdom Heart.

According to the Mahasandhi system, Samantabhadra dwells beyond the characteristics of pure or impure elements. Samantabhadra's characteristics are naturally secret, so even a sublime person cannot see them. But as much as sublime beings have purified their gross elements, which come from obscured mind, they can see his secret essence self-created as the visible mandala of his wisdom qualities. The more the gross elements of sublime beings are purified through the recognition of their own pure secret essence, the more they can recognize that there is no contradiction between the elements, and the closer they come to eventually uniting with their own pure secret essence which is the same, from the beginning, as Samantabhadra. Finally, when they no longer have any gross elements, they are perfectly united with their pure secret essence and have become Samantabhadra.

That is why Samantabhadra sings:

> Oh wonderful Dharma, the exquisite secret essence
>   of all perfect Buddhas,
> All born from unborn, and in being born there is
>   no more born.
> Oh wonderful Dharma, the exquisite secret essence of
>   all perfect Buddhas,
> All ceasing from unceasing, and in ceasing there is no
>   more ceasing.
> Oh wonderful Dharma, the exquisite secret essence
>   of all perfect Buddhas,
> All existing from not existing, and in existing there is
>   no more existing.
> Oh wonderful Dharma, the exquisite secret essence
>   of all perfect Buddhas,
> All coming and going from not coming and going,
>   and in coming and going there is no more coming
>   and going.

Personal and General Phenomena

Things are not what they seem,
nor are they otherwise.
—LORD BUDDHA, *Lankavatara Sutra*

WITHIN RELATIVE TRUTH, there is always circling and reflecting between inner and outer, subtle and gross, subject and object, and personal and general phenomena. If we cannot distinguish between personal and general phenomena, we become confused and cannot make a meaningful connection between subject and object.

An example of personal phenomena is the dream phenomena that arise at night from daytime habits. In a dream we might see a house. Because this is visible only to us, it is our personal phenomenon. Then, we might actually build the house, which becomes visible to all who see it. This is general phenomenon.

General phenomena are the collectively shared, generally visible or objective habits of groups of people or societies. Different expressions of personal phenomena come together to create general phenomena, which in turn leave a residue in further personal phenomena. For example, a fashion designer might introduce a new fashion through his personal phenomena. This becomes general group phenomena, which might inspire another designer, who in turn might create a new derivative fashion.

We trust in general phenomena through agreed-upon complementary gross elements and logic. For example, when we only know white sugar and have never seen brown sugar, we have white sugar's phenomena, and whenever we think of sugar, we automatically think white. We do not even need the word *white* because it is generally agreed upon and assumed. But if somewhere else there are people who only know brown sugar, they do not even need the word *brown* because when they think of sugar they automatically think brown. Those who have both white and brown sugars' habit think, "Which sugar, white or brown?"

Unless our dualistic mind is in the dullness of unconscious mind or until it becomes enlightened nondualistic Wisdom Mind, there will always be obstructed phenomena. Where phenomena are obstructed, there are always true and untrue conceptions; one's truth is another's untruth and one's untruth is another's truth. According to dualistic mind, truth exists temporarily as true or untrue conceptions depending on its relation to intention and circumstances. That is why we call it relative truth.

Within the system of relative truth there are two divisions: actual relative truth and inverted relative truth. These two divisions are not absolute categories but are relative to each other and depend on point of view. For example, to a male tiger, a female tiger is attractive. This is his actual relative truth. To us a tiger is only frightening, and his passion is inverted relative truth.

According to ordinary mind, actual relative truth is what can be perceived through the senses and what functions. In this system, inverted relative truth is a symbol of actual relative truth, like a painting of the moon or its reflection in water, which does not function because it divides the inner invisible from the outer visible elements.

According to sublime mind, the actual relative truth and the inverted relative truth of ordinary mind are both inverted relative truth. For sublime mind, absolute truth is beyond conceptions of inner and outer, so the two truths of ordinary mind are both illusions created by deluded mind, which cannot be relied on for reaching enlightenment.

Personal phenomena's inverted relative truth may be actual relative truth for general phenomena. For example, a magician knows that his magic is not true but creates magic tricks which his naive audience believes to be true. General phenomena's inverted relative truth may be actual relative truth for personal phenomena. For example, Hitler's motivations were lunatic inverted relative truth for many nations, but for him they were intelligent actual relative truth. His actions were actual relative truth for everyone.

Ordinary beings think that desirable qualities are useful. This is their actual relative truth. Hinayana practitioners think that these same qualities are useless and the cause of suffering with no benefit for reaching enlightenment. To them ordinary beings' actual relative truth is inverted relative truth. Hinayana practitioners think that desirable qualities are real and try to abandon them through aversion in order to reach enlightenment. This is their actual relative truth. Mahayana practitioners think that for those who see phenomena as illusory, there is no cause for attachment or aversion, which is a benefit for reaching enlightenment. To them Hinayana's actual relative truth is inverted relative truth. Mahayana practitioners think all desirable and undesirable qualities are illusory. This is their actual relative truth. Inner Vajrayana practitioners think that seeing all qualities as pure deity phenomena is a benefit for reaching enlightenment. To them Mahayana's actual relative truth is inverted relative truth. Inner Vajrayana practitioners think that whatever arises is wisdom display. This is their actual relative truth.

According to the actual relative truth of some modern nihilist scientists, all phenomena are created by chance or accident. But according to the actual relative truth of Buddhism, individual intention creates all personal and general phenomena, and chance or accident is defined as the impure manifestation of previous karma. The karma of personal phenomena takes effect in the same way as a seed planted in unfavorable or favorable conditions. The root circumstance seed has dormant within it receptivity to the contributing circumstances of suitable earth, water, fire, air, and space elements. If they do not all coincide, or one is missing, the seed grows with defects. If they occur together favorably in time and place, the seed grows into a healthy plant. In the same way, if our karma is not good, our root circumstance mind will be attracted to contributing circumstances which are not conducive to a favorable rebirth and we will be reborn with resulting obscurations. If our karma is good, our root circumstance mind all be attracted to contributing circumstances of parents whose genes, qualities, or situation in time and place are conducive to a favorable rebirth.

The karma of personal phenomena also links with contributing circumstances consisting of bad and good general group phenomena, such as mass starvation and genocide or national prosperity and peace. The personal phenomena of people who do not believe in karma often attract bad general group phenomena because it is based on a belief in the ego power of the gross elements. Such people believe that phenomena can be terminated through gross element means and do not believe in the power of the mind to reappear in new visible and invisible forms. They are not afraid of creating negative phenomena with their gross elements in order to achieve their impure intentions which come from the energy of many previous lives' karmic elements.

If they are political leaders, they will attract bad general group phenomena through murder or genocide, trying to purge their country of people they consider to be inferior. On the other hand, political leaders who understand the nature of karma realize that mind never dies and that a country's enemies or negative phenomena cannot be terminated by gross element means such as murder or genocide. Gandhi was such a leader. He understood that positive phenomena should be created with intention, and through his peaceful mind's personal phenomena he tried to create peaceful general phenomena.

Regardless of our political tendencies, we are always suffering back and forth between general and personal phenomena. Sometimes through general phenomena agreement we revolt and liberate ourselves from the personal phenomena of an evil dictator. Then we elect a new leader who creates new general phenomena through his personal phenomena which in time we will want to change again. Whether our phenomena are good or bad, it is the general phenomenon of samsara to be always circling.

Impermanent general phenomena will always change or harm the personal phenomena of an ordinary leader who only believes in the ego power of the gross elements. A sublime person with pure wisdom energy can change general phenomena with his personal phenomena, but he will never harm them. General phenomena can never change or harm his pure personal phenomena because general phenomena's gross impure elements cannot penetrate his pure elements, just as a volcano can never affect the source of the shining sunlight. He has secret egoless wisdom power which is inexhaustible and always benefits because it is light and pure.

Without this pure power, the energy of the subtle elements must depend on the unsteady energy of the gross elements. If we do not recognize our secret essence root circumstances and use the energy of our subtle elements externally on contributing circumstances, then when contributing circumstances diminish, our energy diminishes. Although the energy of our secret root circumstances never diminishes, it can become dormant or hidden through neglect and from not connecting with contributing circumstances, so that this energy is lost to us when we need it.

If we can realize the secret potential of our elements, we can create new contributing circumstances endlessly. Ordinary root circumstances depend on contributing circumstances to develop, but Wisdom Mind's secret root circumstances need no contributing circumstances in order to manifest since they are the pure secret essence. When recognized, they will not diminish or become dormant, even when contributing circumstances change, because they never depend on gross or subtle circumstances. That is why they are called secret.

According to the ordinary logic of samsara, root circumstances and contributing circumstances are always different, but according to sublime logic, contributing circumstances are inherent within root circumstances; one cannot exist without the other, just as light cannot exist without darkness. If this were not so, how could we meet with and accept contributing circumstances?

Through the meeting of good light element contributing circumstances with our good light element root circumstances, the separation between contributing and root circumstances becomes less and less, and spiritual qualities become vaster and lighter. When they have become completely inseparable and root circumstances are not different from contributing circumstances and contributing circumstances are not different from root circumstances, we call this enlightenment.

Until we become enlightened, personal and general phenomena communicate with each other. Because of this communication, it is possible for the personal spiritual qualities of enlightened beings to become conspicuous through their history and to remain like echoes in the general spiritual system even though the source of their pure self-visible phenomena is invisible to us until enlightenment. For individuals as well as for groups, when the contributing circumstance, the sublime history of enlightened beings, joins with the root circumstance, our secret essence enlightenment seed, the seed can awaken and grow. By the joining of these two circumstances, our spiritual qualities increase.

When we remember great sublime beings such as Milarepa, Jesus, Buddha Shakyamuni, and Padmasambhava, we think they performed miracles intentionally. Of course, it is good to feel this way because by trying to connect with their pure secret essence we accumulate merit. But the perception of this intention is only our general group phenomena agreement. Actually these miracles only appeared when sublime beings used the pure undivided secret essence of the elements, which exists from the beginning, in order to make truth conspicuous.

We think they were performing miracles and creating magic because we are limited by our gross elements obscurations and do not believe in what we cannot do ourselves. So when according to general group phenomena agreement it is said that Jesus walked on the water, we believe it is a miracle because our obscured dualistic mind divides the elements between water and earth. According to the personal phenomena of Jesus, he was not walking on the water. With his equanimity mind, he was only remaining in the primordial secret essence of the elements, which is never divided, always vast, inseparably pervading everywhere. According to the division habit perception of general group phenomena, a pure event is made impure because we obscure the relative truth of Jesus by separating it from the absolute truth of Jesus. When it is said that Jesus walked on the water, it means that through the contributing circumstances of this history, he was adapting to individual faculties and encouraging beings to increase their spiritual qualities.

The gross and subtle elements are always connected to their secret essence. People who saw Jesus walking on the water had a good karmic link with him because with their gross and subtle elements' phenomena, they could connect to the pure secret essence of what they perceived as a miracle. Even now, when we hear through the history of our elements' unbroken lineage that Jesus walked on the water, we are using our gross and subtle elements' phenomena to know about the pure secret essence phenomena of Jesus.

The Buddha said, "I show you the path of liberation; it depends on you whether or not you attain liberation." This means that without trying to find liberation through inward examination, we cannot recognize the truth within our personal phenomena, whose source is the pure secret essence of the elements. Still we try to find liberation only through outward examination and hope to recognize the truth in our general group phenomena, whose source is the gross elements. If we think we can benefit our personal phenomena by developing general phenomena's gross elements, we have not realized that we cannot rely on gross elements' phenomena because they are impermanent and will change. When the outer elements become inflexible and inert and diminish, our undeveloped personal phenomena seem hopeless. Then, because of our lack of confidence in the pure source of our personal phenomena, we blame general phenomena and say that Dharma is false. In this way, through inexperience with the secret pure essence of the elements, we create negative phenomena towards general phenomena and never love or have faith in ourselves. But if we first recognize and establish confidence in our own personal phenomena's pure secret essence and light energy, we can love and have faith in ourselves because we understand clearly that the never-fading, never-diminishing source of all pure qualities is our Wisdom Mind. Then, we are automatically self-conquered by the pure self-seduction of the five Wisdom Dakinis, who rule the universal five elements and are the consorts of the five Wisdom Buddhas. Through this self-evidence, through the spontaneous endless increase of our spiritual qualities, we can spontaneously generate positive phenomena towards general phenomena, which become pure through our own pure view.

If we do not have this pure wisdom point of view, whether we practice with yoga, rituals, visualization, or meditation according to our personal phenomena faculties, we only remain in gross element samsara. If we practice according to pure Dharma, it does not matter whether we have negative or positive conceptions since both can be dissolved into equanimity mind. When negative does not have solid negative essence and positive does not have solid positive essence, both appear only as display. Then samsaric reality phenomena dissolve and there is no longer even the name samsara. Only with a wisdom point of view can we transform our personal impure gross element self-phenomena into pure self-secret wisdom phenomena. Since all general phenomena come from personal phenomena, when personal phenomena become pure, impure general phenomena also become pure. Through this transformation, we can spontaneously help beings without rejecting general phenomena and without accepting personal phenomena, becoming one with the pure secret essence of all phenomena.

The Two Extremes and Beyond
the Two Extremes

Suffering in hopefulness is the eternalist.
Suffering in hopelessness is the nihilist.
Beyond both hopefulness and hopelessness
is the Buddhist.

BECAUSE of our habits, we do not recognize the pure secret wisdom potential of the five senses, which is inseparable from the pure secret wisdom potential of the five elements. Instead we use the gross internal senses, which perceive only the gross external elements, and we can only understand the divisionless secret essence of phenomena as separated and divided and substantial. If we value substance as most long-lasting and immutable and, after gross phenomena vanish, we conclude that the subtle elements remain as its most refined and pure aspect, this is the basis of the eternalist point of view. If we value nothing beyond conspicuous substance and, when gross phenomena vanish, we conclude that nothing else exists beyond substance, this is the basis of the nihilist point of view. In either case we never believe in the secret essence which pervades and continues beyond both visible and subtle elements.

Eternalism is expressed by many different people in many different ways, but essentially, they share the point of view that a subtler form exists beyond the visible and tangible elements. Eternalists believe in an everlasting immortal deity whose infinite subtle qualities are the source of the gross substance elements. They believe that those who trust and pray to a primordial creator of heaven and earth will temporarily obtain benefit in this life and ultimately have immortal life after their gross element body dies. They believe that when the gross elements disappear, the subtle element soul is reborn as a god or in the retinue of a god in an eternal heaven or pureland beyond the gross elements. Eternalists usually worship deities who appeared on the earth in legendary times and whose qualities are revealed through their subtle element history. They worship countless different images of deities in as many different forms as there are traditions to benefit beings.

Nihilism is expressed by many different people in many different ways, but essentially they share the point of view that there is nothing beyond the substance qualities of the gross elements. They do not believe in a substanceless source of the gross elements. Some believe that substance appears out of nothing, and others believe in the inexhaustible circle of matter and energy, that phenomena arise when circumstances gather by chance and coincidence. According to the nihilists' point of view, when the elements come together, the gross element form of the body is born spontaneously, combined inseparably with the mind. They believe that when the gross elements have separated and dissolved, only ashes remain, and there is nothing left of the mind. So the nihilists have no need for conceptions of a future life or a continuous karmic connection. Nihilists usually revere qualities of power, fame, beauty, progress, and success, and are attached to gross elements in countless different forms, through countless different worldly ways depending on their culture's gross element history, to benefit themselves in this life in as many styles as there are worldly egos.

To the eternalist, the nihilist's reliance only on gross substance is a threat to the understanding of the subtle substance source of all phenomena. To the nihilist, the eternalist's reliance on the subtle and immaterial is a threat to material progress, which is the visible product of all substantial qualities.

Eternalists actually believe in the pure essence of the elements even though they would not express it in terms of the elements. They understand that there can be no permanent connection between the impermanent gross elements, so when they pray they rely on the benefit of their pure elements. By desiring to know their god, to obtain his power, blessing, or grace, to gain immortality in a pureland or heaven, eternalists are trying to reach the pure essence of the elements. They are really saying that the impure gross element form of the object of worship can connect with the pure light form of the object of worship in this life, and that after the gross elements have become inert and have perished, the pure essence remains fresh and eternal. This unacknowledged belief in the pure elements is expressed through countless forms of prayers, whether with offerings of repellent blood, clear water, or beautiful flowers, whether in traditional style, in hopeful and entreating praise, or with lonely lamentations. It is expressed through prayers whether the deity is in the form of a beast with tails, horns, or wings, or in human or superhuman form, whether the aspect is cruel or kind, wrathful or peaceful, violent or comforting, whether the deity is riding an animal or dancing in the sky, whether crucified or sitting on a stainless lotus, whether on a shining moon or sun or on a jeweled throne, the essence of all such devotion is always the pure source of the elements.

Light pure form appears unobstructedly and inseparably from stainless emptiness; form cannot arise in dull nothingness. Deity's form cannot appear, deity's speech cannot sound, deity's mind cannot pervade in the gross elements without a pure element intention. The grace and blessing of the deity's form come predominantly from the pure earth and water elements; the grace and blessing of the deity's speech come predominantly from the pure fire and air elements; the grace and blessing of the deity's mind come predominantly from the pure space element.

Nihilists are also actually involved with the substanceless source of all substance, although they would deny it. As the Buddha said, "Buddha nature pervades all sentient beings." Although nihilists say that the subtle elements do not exist, they describe people's temperaments as earthy, watery, fiery, airy, and spacey, and use such expressions as down-to-earth, icy indifference, dampened spirits, heated discussion, hot-blooded, stormy-tempered, and open-minded.

If we ask nihilist government leaders whether they believe in the invisible subtle qualities of phenomena, they will say no, yet their police and soldiers are always calculating in the visible present for invisible future events and making plans based on something invisible and subtle that will become visible and gross in the future. This means they actually do believe that the invisible and subtle exist. Although nihilists say that they do not believe in karma, by their planning they reveal their belief in the invisible continuity between the past and the future and their belief in causing future results. This believing in cause and result means implicitly that they also believe in karma.

The intention of nihilists is similar to the intention of some meditators. If we ask a formless meditator what he is meditating on, he might answer: "Nothing with form, nothing visible." Yet he really wants to catch the invisible, to see something special; otherwise, what is he waiting for? If he catches something, he behaves like government police. First, they make the invisible visible; then, they try to change or annihilate it. When you ask the nihilist and the meditator if their intention is the same, they will deny it; but really it is the same.

If we ask a nihilist what time it is, he might answer that it is one o'clock. Then if we ask him what he is going to do this afternoon, he might say he has an appointment at five o'clock. This implies that he believes in the subtle invisible elements dormant in time expressed as the future, so his response is based on the belief in a future life even though he would deny believing in it if he were asked directly.

Nihilists think that they are separated from the external elements by their physical bodies, but actually the secret essence of all elements which pervades all phenomena is never divided. Even if one person is in Paris telephoning another in New York, there is really no separation. Even though we think that mind is inside our bodies, it is really neither inside nor outside, neither in our brain nor in our heart. If we carefully examine this "inside and outside," we cannot find the limits of inside and outside. Our limit comes from the karmic habit of using gross elements, which create these divisions between New York and Paris, between one voice and another, between inside and outside. All divisions come from these karmic gross element habits.

Two people can connect with each other from a long distance and communicate their minds' subtle thoughts with their subtle, untouchable voices through the gross apparatus of the telephone. Even though they are already linked from the beginning through their all-pervading linkless mind, dormant subtle elements are awakened through the gross circumstances of the telephone call, and their original connection is remade. But we had better not tell nihilist telephone engineers about this all-pervading, secret, linkless link or they will want to cut the gross metal telephone wires.

Our real mind is limitless, but we do not know it because we only use our limited ordinary minds. When we think of the telephone call, our minds stop at Paris, at New York, and between Paris and New York. Through our subtle elements we can easily remember a country we have been to before because of our previous link with its gross elements, but because we remain in our divided gross elements, we cannot go beyond this limit. If through our subtle elements, we imagine a country we have never visited, or if we dream of a country where we have never been, it may mean we have been there in a previous life or will be there in the future, but even this unknown country conception is the subtle limit of our ordinary minds. Whenever we stay in the extreme of nihilism or in the extreme of eternalism, we divide phenomena from emptiness, and because of our division habit, we cannot go beyond into the pure light secret essence of the elements.

The Buddha is beyond eternalism and never remains in any elements. The Buddha is beyond nihilism and never separates from any elements. But sentient beings cannot recognize this, so we always trust either eternalism or nihilism and are always suffering and punishing ourselves in the circle of death and rebirth.

That is why the Buddha aimlessly manifests as certain deities with eternal qualities and aspects, such as never dying and always pure, in order to release beings obscured by nihilist misunderstandings. That is also why the nature of the Buddha's manifestations is said to be emptiness in order to release beings obscured by eternalist misunderstandings. Actually the Buddha pervades in both extremes inseparably, and therefore remains beyond both extremes. He never remains in either extreme as deity or emptiness because they are inseparable. Separating deity from emptiness or emptiness from deity creates ordering and circling from one extreme to the other. Buddhism is beyond these two extremes.

Buddhism is the point of view that follows Buddha's words. Whenever we have a point of view, we have subject and object and between subject and object. If we stay in a bungalow, we can only see the view in front of us, but not above us. If we stay on the top of a high building, we can only see the view in front of us, around us, and below us, including the bungalow. If we stay on the top of a mountain peak, we can see the view of what is in front of us, around us, and below us, and everything in between, including the bungalow and the high building. Depending on our faculties which come from previous karmic phenomena, we are able to see one point of view or many different points of view. Even though we hear about something which we cannot see, often we cannot accept it because of our individual faculties and our limited point of view habit.

For countless lives we may try to find our mind, but it can never be found within any substance phenomena because it is always great emptiness. This point of view goes beyond the eternalist point of view without rejecting it. Our mirror mind always reflects countless phenomena unobstructedly and effortlessly. This point of view goes beyond the nihilist point of view without rejecting it. This does not mean that great emptiness and unobstructed phenomena exist separately and can be combined together like two threads being twisted to make one. From the beginning, emptiness and phenomena are inseparable. This is the general Buddhist point of view. Wherever there is emptiness, there are phenomena, and wherever there are phenomena, there is emptiness. We do not see this because of our dualistic mind division habit, so we only view things one at a time, seeing emptiness as different from phenomena. Sometimes instead of recognizing our inherent pervading emptiness mind, when we practice we try to create a different emptiness, and when we cannot find it or are unable to create it through our phenomena, we become frustrated.

From ordinary beings to sublime beings, point of view exists until enlightenment is reached. Within the Buddhist point of view, depending on different individual faculties, there are different points of view.

According to the Hinayana system, the point of view is egolessness. According to the Mahayana system, the point of view is egolessness, the insubstantiality of phenomena, and freedom from all mental activities. According to the Mahamudra system, the point of view is all-pervasive Wisdom Mind in existent and nonexistent phenomena. According to the Mahasandhi system, the point of view is the beginningless liberation of Samantabhadra's Wisdom Mind.

In enlightened Wisdom Mind, there is no subject, no object, no between subject and object, no beginning, no end, no time, and no direction, so there is no point of view.

The Buddha said, "Even though I did not appear anywhere, I appear everywhere to those who like appearance. To those who do not like appearance, I am always emptiness.

"Even though I have never spoken, I speak to those who like sound. To those who do not like sound, I remain silent.

"Even though my mind has never thought anything, to those who think my mind is omniscient, it is omniscient. To those who think my mind does not exist, it does not exist.

"Whoever wants to see me gradually can see me gradually. Whoever wants to see me instantly can see me instantly. Whatever is wished for will be attained. This is the quality of my body.

"Whoever wants to hear me gradually can hear me gradually. Whoever wants to hear me instantly can hear me instantly. Whatever is wished for will be attained. This is the quality of my speech.

"Whoever wants to know my mind gradually can know my mind gradually. Whoever wants to know my mind instantly can know my mind instantly. Whatever is wished for will be attained. This is the quality of my mind."

Lineage

The teaching of the whispered lineage
is the Dakini's breath.

—MILAREPA

ESSENCE LINEAGE is the unbreakable natural connection with continuous pure and natural energy. If we separate natural energy from its secret source, it becomes obscured and impure and then lineage appears broken. When our subtle elements become gross, obscured by the five skandhas, the pure essence of the elements seems diminished or lost, but really it has only become hidden. Everything visible has invisible essence. Even cement, which seems completely gross and inert, has invisible natural essence. The substanceless source of the elements pervades all subtle and gross phenomena, even though when we have broken lineage, what is visible seems only a lifeless remainder.

When we eat fresh natural food which comes from visible gross elements, it connects with subtle elements to produce invisible energy, but inert visible excrement still remains. When we sleep, our gross elements' waking phenomena connect with our subtle elements to produce invisible excrement in the form of dreams. When we are born, previous lives' karma connects with present life's circumstances, resulting in this life's dream situations. In each case, what remains seems inert because it is divided from its invisible source and its essence lineage appears broken. Excrement is the residue of this broken lineage.

The fresher something is, the closer it is to its natural source and its natural lineage. The older food gets, the more stale and inert it is, and the less accessible its secret essence is to us when we eat it. Our phenomena are constantly in the process of becoming stale and inert unless, through practice, we can return them to freshness. Our body is constantly in the process of becoming inert unless, through practice, we can return it to the Youthful Vase Body.

Youth is symbolic of pure balance in Dharma because the secret essence of the elements manifests visibly in things when they are young and their subtle and gross elements are in balance. When a tree is young, its leaves display pure light and fresh colors because its branches, roots, and leaves absorb and use earth, water, fire, air, and space in balance with each other. When sentient beings are young, their bodies are light and their complexion is fresh because they sustain their body from the earth's food, blood from water, warmth from the sun's fire, breath from air, and consciousness from mind's space, in balance with each other. As living things grow older, an imbalanced relationship develops between the subtle and gross elements, which are dependent on each other. Some of the elements become more dominant and conspicuous while others become weaker and dormant. Trees produce heavy, inert bark and the human body produces inert fingernails, hair, pus, and mucus. The leaves of the trees become brittle and colorless, people's complexions become dry and pale, until finally the connection between the gross and subtle elements becomes so imbalanced that it completely breaks, leaving a dead tree or a corpse as an inert remainder. For those who are able to go beyond the obstructed gross and subtle elements to their unobstructed secret essence, there is no imbalance, and so no inert gross elements are left behind. They leave a rainbow body, the pure color essence of the visible elements.

When we cannot go beyond into the substanceless and our substance lineage can only be traced to a subtle substance particle limit, which this generation temporarily calls a quark, but perhaps another generation in the future will name differently to mark a new subtle substance limit, this is the deluded mind lineage of samsara. If we continuously recognize the secret essence which pervades all phenomena, there is natural unbroken Wisdom Mind lineage, which is unobstructed and without end. Lineage means the continuous, unbroken precious qualities manifested through many different forms and aspects, whose essence always remains pure.

According to the Vinaya, there are seven discipline lineage holders of the Buddha Shakyamuni. According to Bodhichitta lineage holders through Manjushri and Maitreya, there are Six Ornaments and Two Excellences. According to the Tantric tradition, the lineage holders are the eight-four Mahasiddhas or saints. According to the Nyingma system, there are the Buddha's wisdom transmission and the sublime beings' oral transmission.

If we are not connected to our secret essence Wisdom Mind because we are obscured by tradition, race, nationality, rank, or politics, we cannot know pure Buddhist lineage. Some Easterners, or Westerners who think like Easterners, believe that Westerners cannot have lineage because they have no tradition. If we believe that Westerners are too materialistic to have any spiritual lineage, we are disrespectful to pure Buddhist lineage. If we are not concerned with true spiritual qualities but are superficially seduced by Eastern customs and manners because we associate the East with Buddhist lineage, we are also disrespectful to pure Buddhist lineage. If we think that only priests, lamas, and gurus have lineage, then we have title lineage conception and padlock and key lineage conception which is disrespectful to pure spiritual lineage.

There are many holy places in the East which the Buddha Shakyamuni blessed. If we do not respect these places, we are disrespectful to pure Buddhist lineage. Some people have the conception that only Indians have Buddhist lineage because the Buddha Shakyamuni was born in India or that whoever comes from Bethlehem has Jesus' lineage. But the Buddha said that real teaching never depends on race. If we do not acknowledge those who hold pure lineage regardless of where they come from, we are disrespectful to vast omniscient spiritual lineage.

If we practice Dharma depending on ordinary substance lineage power, we cannot have deep spiritual power. The source of visible power is always invisible power. For example, some machines are very powerful, but we cannot see or touch the electricity that runs them because the source of its power is invisible. If we cannot connect visible substance power to its invisible substanceless source, then it is quickly exhausted. This is especially true today when Easterners and Westerners are making Dharma factories, trying to bargain with substance lineage for power and gain. Like capitalists who want prestige and wealth in order to have the respect of others, we want gain that is touchable and useful and are afraid of poverty, anonymity, and loss of worldly power. We think that lineage must be exclusive, only for those who accumulate spiritual prestige. We think that lineage is found only through associating with conspicuously high people, well-known Dharma centers, and teachers who have been recognized by the public as traditional lineage holders.

We may pretend to be Buddhists, but if we do not have a wisdom point of view and the compassion that the Buddha Shakyamuni revealed again and again, then whatever Dharma acts we perform are just Dharma drama for the nihilist audience to senselessly gossip about during intermission.

Some people think lineage depends on a teacher. Especially some Easterners believe that Westerners cannot have lineage because they are not linked from birth to a spiritual teacher. Unless we are nihilists and believe only in the visible, we cannot judge the spiritual qualities of someone who has no visible teacher in this life. If someone takes water from the tap, because we have not seen them take it from the source, is this reason to say it is not water? On a pilgrimage, pilgrims need a guide at first, but when they know the path, they can go alone. In the end, just because they have no visible guide, we cannot say they do not know the path. Of course, for most people lineage depends on a visible teacher, and, in general, if we can find a good teacher it is necessary to have a guide. But according to the Buddhist tradition, if we believe in karma, we believe that because some people had a visible teacher in previous lives and have experience with the pure essence of their elements, they can be reborn to become enlightened without depending on a visible teacher in this life. Even if we have one hundred teachers, if we separate from our natural mind, we have broken lineage. Even if we have no teacher, when we are connected to our natural mind, we have true Wisdom Mind lineage.

Our ordinary mind is deluded mind, so our eyes are definitely deluded. Even though it seems to be reality, what we see is probably a hallucination, as a person with jaundice sees a white conch as yellow. So we cannot say that this one has lineage or that one does not. This only creates obscurations about pure lineage. If we want to talk about pure Dharma lineage, we must be concerned with purity. Buddha Shakyamuni said, "My fearless lion's Dharma throne does not have an owner. The one who has compassion, who has Wisdom Mind, who has a benefitting mind, this one is the older of my lineage and can sit upon my throne." He did not say the one who has a title, the one who is chosen by neurotic-minded people, the one who has created more politics. Whether one is titled or untitled, chosen or not chosen, politician or not politician, the lineage holder is the one who has original wisdom qualities and whose mind source is wisdom purity. Whoever has vast spiritual qualities through pure intention and gifted mind from previous karma holds a pure spiritual lineage and can truly benefit other beings.

> Even though born the daughter of a noble family,
> You found no essence in such worldly life,
> So you ran from your splendid castle
> And wandered from place to place
> Seeking only ultimate liberation.

> At the time you looked for liberation,
> With your incomparably exquisite form blossoming,
> Two princes sought to make you their princess,
> But in the midst of their disputes
> You became queen

> Of the most powerful monarch,
> Manifestation of sunrise-colored prajna body,
> Raising the sword of stainless awareness,
> Cutting through nets of ignorance.

Even though with the supreme ruler
You became queen of the land,
Surrounded by a snow mountain rosary,
You were utterly free of attachment.

When your most wondrous betrothed
Offered you to the vagabond Acharya,
You recognized him as no ordinary being
But the very glowing of Amitabha,
And so you merged your mind with his wisdom heart.

To you, Yeshe Tsogyal, I bow always
Until I become the same as you.

Habit, Dream, and Time

My form appeared like a dream
to sentient beings who are like a dream.
I taught them dreamlike teaching to attain
  dreamlike enlightenment.
  —LORD BUDDHA, *Supreme Jewel Mound*

FROM beginningless time there are no habits in unconditioned natural mind. Still we create habit by dividing phenomena from clear space. Inherently a mirror does not have any dust. Still it attracts and gathers dust, which obscures its natural clarity. In the same way, our pure Wisdom Mind becomes obscured by ego when we become attached to its pure phenomena's unobstructed display. If we can recognize our natural stainless mind, we will not become obscured through attachment, but if we do not recognize our pure natural mind, then our subtle elements' phenomena gather like dust on our clear mirror mind.

If we wipe away light particle dust immediately, we can easily clean a mirror. If a habit is in its seed stage, we can easily make it vanish. But when we leave a mirror without cleaning it, subtle particles gather, attracting heavier particles which stick to them until the mirror becomes completely obscured and very difficult to clean. If we are careless and neglect our inconspicuous subtle element habits, they become the cause of gross heavy conspicuous habits.

Our conspicuous easily recognizable habits are like the mold which appears on stale food. Our subtle inconspicuous habits are like the fire under hot ashes. When we purify our mind, we must remove all residual habits, no matter how subtle they are. If we leave just one speck of dust on our mirror mind, this is still residual habit. Even if we have only one conception left, only one phenomenon, whether good or bad, it is still residual habit which obscures. Clouds, whether they are black or white, are still clouds which obscure.

The heavy element habits of ordinary beings are like the thick musk in the gland of a musk deer. The light element habits of sublime beings before enlightenment are like the subtle residual odor after the musk has been removed that persists for a time before it completely disappears. Ordinary beings have gross pain and gross happiness from their gross element habits. Some Bodhisattvas still have pain and happiness, but because it comes from their light element habits, it is like a thin residue compared to the thick root habit pain and happiness of ordinary beings. Some Bodhisattvas express pain only to reveal the truth of karma and to purify that karma for suffering sentient beings by demonstrating weariness of samsara.

Inherently, pure basic earth has no growth. Through elements' circumstances, growth appears and obscures the earth. Habits are like growth. Inherently, pure basic water has no mire. Through elements' circumstances, mire appears and obscures the water. Habits are like mire. Inherently, pure basic fire has no smoke. Through elements' circumstances, smoke appears and obscures the fire. Habits are like smoke. Inherently, pure basic air has no dust. Through elements' circumstances, dust appears and obscures the air. Habits are like dust. Inherently, pure basic sky has no clouds. Through elements' circumstances, clouds appear and obscure the sky. Habits are like clouds.

Mind is like pure limitless ground. If we are not attracted to and do not cling to our finite limited phenomena, then we can remain in our fresh boundless mind. Mind is like pure clear water. If we are not attracted to and do not cling to our murky phenomena, then we can remain in our naturally pristine mind. Mind is like pure radiant fire. If we are not attracted to and do not cling to our smoky phenomena, then we can remain in our light luminous mind. Mind is like pure weightless air. If we are not attracted to and do not cling to our dusty phenomena, then we can remain in our unobstructed clear mind. Mind is like pure stainless sky. If we are not attracted to and do not cling to our cloudy phenomena, then we can remain in our open space mind.

Habits manifest at all times, waking and sleeping. In our ordinary mind, visible daytime habit phenomena are gross and invisible dreamtime habit phenomena are subtle. But the subtle element is always present in the gross element, so in the true practitioner's mind, daytime habit phenomena are not different from dreamtime habit phenomena.

Our invisible dream habit phenomena are like stars which we cannot see while the sky is lit up by the daytime sun, but still they are there. Gross daytime phenomena do not make subtle dream phenomena vanish. Our ordinary mind's impure invisible dream habits do not vanish until we make our impure visible waking habits vanish. Even though from beginningless time there is nothing visible, still we always create and believe the unbelievable visible. Between visible and invisible we are always suffering. As Shantideva said, "A sterile woman does not have a child, yet in her dream her child is dead and she is suffering." But for the true practitioner who understands the pure essence of the elements, there is no more gross daytime habit and no more subtle dreamtime habit.

According to the Tantric system, it is not necessary to examine the dreams we have at dark and before midnight, because these dreams are only expressions of previous habits. It is not necessary to examine dreams we have at midnight, when our dreamtime subtle impure elements' conception and our daytime gross impure elements' conception are connected, since they create disturbances which manifest themselves as demons. We should examine dreams we have at dawn if we want to know the future.

If we have a bad dream, we can dispel its negative phenomena through prayer and meditation. If it is a good dream, we can keep its positive phenomena through prayer and meditation and it might come true. If we practice formless meditation and want to rest within Equanimity Wisdom Mind, we should recognize that it is not important whether or not dreams come true because daytime and dreamtime are both a dream. We should have neither bad feelings and fears about bad dreams nor good feelings and expectations about good dreams, but should try to dissolve our conceptions into luminous space.

If we are using form in our meditation and want to create subtle elements' pure phenomena, then we use dream practice whose essence is to visualize the deity with whom we have a karmic link, according to the sadhana of our individual faculties. If our daytime habit is deity phenomena, our dreamtime habit will become deity phenomena. Gradually impure dream phenomena will transform into pure dream phenomena until ultimately daytime and dreamtime become one pure measureless sphere of Wisdom Deity phenomena.

Our dreamlike daytime and dreamtime habits do not exist apart from circumstances. In the cold shimmering highlands people have the habit of wearing heavy wool and animal furs. In the warm grassy lowlands people have the habit of wearing silk and cotton. When the highlanders descend to the lowlands, their heavy woolen habit still remains and when the lowlanders climb to the highlands, their light cotton habit still remains. Thinking of our sublime deity, even if we try, we cannot see her face. Yet without trying, our own ordinary lover's face spontaneously appears before us. Habits follow wherever we go, and changing our habits remains the greatest difficulty.

It is always very difficult and painful to move from an old familiar place to a new unfamiliar place. It is very difficult to change. Whenever we say "change," we mean changing habits. All cultures, traditions, and religions teach us to change negative habits into positive habits. If we do not want to create negative habits, we must try to destroy them from the beginning. If we see a speckled snake and are afraid, we must try to destroy this fear immediately or we will be afraid when we see a speckled rope because we have become deluded by our speckled snake habit.

One person's positive habit is another person's negative habit, and one person's negative habit is another person's positive habit.

Habit, Dream, and Time

Agreement or disagreement between parents and children, men and women, students and teachers, or governments and their people always arises because they are trying to change negative habits into positive habits according to their own point of view. According to the Dharma point of view, the purpose of all practice and teachings is to purify ego's habits in order to change negative phenomena into positive phenomena.

Our phenomena are always changing within time, and the source of our time habit is substance. As the elements become more gross and substantial, direction begins. As there is more and more direction, there is more and more time. We cannot see all time at once because our present-tense mind is caught in the gross substance elements. We cannot see past-tense substance because we are divided between the new substance which our mind is always creating and past-tense substance which has become inert. We cannot see future-tense substance because it is not yet ripened or conspicuous. Karma is dormant past and future time, which becomes conspicuous as the present.

Ordinary mind is always divided by time, as ordinary persons' space is divided by the boundaries of gross substance. Because of this, we cannot see beyond the present through the gross elements. It is like being inside a thick solid wall through which we cannot see or penetrate because we are obstructed by substance time.

Bodhisattvas, gifted through karma with sublime qualities, can see all times as if through clear glass. Because they have less gross element obscurations, they can see the future beyond substance. The Buddha, who remains everywhere without remaining anywhere, can see unobstructedly and spontaneously without intention because his elements are beyond substance and his mind is never divided by time. The example of a glass wall cannot even be used. Those who remain in clear space sky mind with all elements in equanimity can see all time and space because it is open and unobstructed. They do not have direction or time because they are neither inside substance nor outside substance. In the sky there are no mountains, no obstacles, no substance obscurations, no direction.

The Buddha sees everything because in Wisdom Mind there is

no time and no direction. Without time and direction, there is nothing more to see. But if there is nothing more to see, how can the Buddha be a guide and benefit sentient beings? If we think there is no time, how can the Buddha predict time? If we think there is no direction, how can the Buddha indicate direction?

The Buddha is omniscient; his mind is like the sky. He does not show anything; what appears is a reflection. If sentient beings have direction, it is reflected. If sentient beings have time, it is reflected. So really time is not a reflection of the Buddha, it is a reflection of us. If we open a parasol in the sky, a shadow comes back to the earth. Substance elements appear in the same way. Time comes back like a shadow to our body, so time is our own phenomenon.

In order to have external agreement, certain time is derived from general phenomena time through observations and judgments based on conspicuous, gross, external elements and conditions. When these elements are generally complementary, we make clocks to show the same time, maps to show the same direction in space, and histories to show the same direction in time. Astrologers make time calendars through the stars, scientists through computers, and roosters through their inner element senses. Time seems more and more true through general group rooster and scientist agreement, but sometimes scientists' computers break down, creating errors, and sometimes roosters crow in their sleep because of a dawn habit dream. We must know that there is no one single general phenomena time agreement. As the full moon sinks behind the western mountains with a greeting beam of light to the mountain peak in the east, simultaneously, the sun rises from behind the eastern mountains with a farewell ray of light to the mountain peak in the west.

In the East, according to one of the traditions of astrology, one breath from a healthy adult body is comprised of three steps: inhalation, retention, and exhalation of air. Six breaths are called a chusang, and there are sixty chusang in one hour and sixty hours in a day and a night. All calculations are based on this particular chusang day and night conception. In the North, Alaskans have Alaskans' time agreement of uneven hours of daytime and nighttime, while in the South, inhabitants of tropical countries are accustomed to even hours of daytime and nighttime. Everywhere, time is very fickle since it is within substance and it is always changing and becoming inert. If we try to make it exact while relying on impermanent substance, we become frustrated and crazy.

We cannot depend on external time and direction because, according to karma, the elements of each individual are different and therefore the quality of time within them is different. For this reason we show time through our substance elements in different ways. Some of us are foggy and always want to sleep, some of us cannot sleep as quickly as others, and some of us wake up earlier than others. When the elements are light and subtle, the quality of time within them is moderate, smooth, and even. When the elements are heavy and gross, the quality of time within them is rough and uneven, sometimes fast, sometimes slow. When people with different elements meet, the interaction between them can be either turbulent or harmonious depending in part on whether the qualities of time within their elements are complementary. If two people meet and the quality of the time within their elements is even and moderate, they are always in harmony. If their elements are uneven, they can be in harmony with each other only when the qualities of time within their elements synchronize. When their time qualities do not correspond, they interact turbulently.

All human beings depend on time in their daily activities to communicate. But even though we depend on time, we often cannot connect with each other. For instance, sometimes through different time habits within our elements we cannot meet even though we think we have made a certain time appointment. When we miss the time, we never think the energies of our different personal time element habits are incompatible. We just say, "I am sorry. I am late." When someone is prompt, we say, "Oh, how nice, you're right on time." And between "I am sorry, I am late" and "Oh, how nice, you're right on time," we can spend all our life's time.

Temporarily, practitioners must depend on ordinary certain time because we have ordinary element time habits. But ultimately, through meditation, all outer general gross elements and certain time phenomena appear to be inverted relative truth time. This is because by practicing, we develop some experience with no-certain-time phenomena, which are more expansive, permeated by the lineage of timeless time. Then no-certain-time phenomena appear to be actual relative truth. As practitioners continue to practice with these no-certain-time phenomena, past, present, and future time phenomena, inverted relative truth time phenomena, actual relative truth time phenomena, dreamtime and waking time phenomena, all our time habit phenomena ultimately become one time within spaceless space. Then we can always remain in the equanimity of timeless time.

Playmind

Fish play in the water.
Birds play in the sky.
Ordinary beings play on the earth.
Sublime beings play in display.

ONE PERSON'S PLAY is another person's seriousness, and one person's seriousness is another person's play. To adults, adolescents seem playful, but to adolescents, their own phenomena are serious. To adolescents, children seem playful, but to children, their own phenomena are serious. This is because, for countless previous lives, all deluded beings with divided mind have separated phenomena into gross and subtle elements, thinking their play is serious because they believe it is true.

When children are immature and cannot connect their subtle element minds with their gross element toys, they become serious. If they are unable to understand how things work, they develop a frustrated anger habit which they carry into their adult life, changing the object of their frustration from a toy to a person. If from birth they would recognize that play is playful and not serious, and that gross and subtle are inseparable, children and adults would never have frustration or anger.

Separation is always the cause of frustration. Whether between parents and child, friend and friend, husband and wife, or teacher and disciple, when we cannot connect with each other because of our previous habit of dividing subject from object and gross from subtle, frustration and anger result. When we feel this frustration and anger, we must try to dispel it, not by further dividing the object of our frustrated anger, but by practicing Dharma and by meditating.

Even without meditating or using any Dharma conceptions, spiritual qualities exist from the beginning. Spiritual energy is like a young natural forest, which can be burned away through frustrated anger. Like fire, when frustrated anger becomes heavier and heavier, light spiritual energy diminishes like smoke. After the fire, both gross element energy and subtle element energy are exhausted and only the gray ashes of empty sadness remain. Then, lacking support from worldly gross elements and from inner subtle elements, our mind becomes weak and sorrowful.

But through play, spiritual energy can be sustained, so we must not think that play is always bad. Whether or not our rigid mature minds reject play, everything is still the display of the natural secret essence of the elements. If we are serious and rigid, our subtle elements become congested and cannot reflect this wisdom display. If our mind is calm and vast and playful, we can always recognize this essence display. In open space, there is never turbulence between the gross and subtle elements.

When we study, if we have an open playmind, we can absorb what we study. Flexibility comes from playmind, so when our mind is open we can accept what we are taught. We cannot learn with a rigid and serious mind because it is tight and unbalanced. Our serious mind is always tired, while our playmind is always rested. When there is no space and no rest, whatever we learn will be limited

When we work, if we have open playmind, we will not have fear of losing anything, so we can work continuously until we attain our goal. With the confidence that comes from playmind, we never hesitate and do not make mistakes. Doubts and hesitations come from a mind that is too rigidly serious. When we have fears or hesitations, our interest in our work diminishes and we become lazy and weak, losing our confidence. If we do not have confidence, whatever we do, whatever we say, misses the target. Because our mind is scattered and frightened and hesitant, our concentration becomes lost. If we do not have concentration, we cannot penetrate to the target because our mind is always stuck before it reaches its aim. When we realize that we have missed the target, we become frustrated. Our mind becomes even more narrow, unstable, and fragile from this frustration and everything is lost in our life situation.

Without playmind, even if we see beautiful things, we cannot make contact with them because we have fear and miss the target through our lack of confidence. Even if we write, everything is a mistake because we have fear and miss the target through our lack of confidence. Even if we read, we cannot absorb the meaning because we have fear and miss the target through our lack of confidence. Even though we are entertained by friends, the taste does not linger because we have fear and miss the target through our lack of confidence. Even though we seek the company of vast-minded people, they cannot trust us or talk to us since our rigid minds are too small because we have fear and miss the target through our lack of confidence.

If we want to fight someone, we cannot win when our mind is too serious and narrow. Even if we scream and kick and yell, if our mind is rigid we have no power. Our mind becomes scattered and nervous from tension, unable to penetrate its object. In a debate, logic becomes disordered in a rigid, crowded mind since thoughts are scattered and there is no open space in which the mind can play. So if we are too serious and tense, we will always be defeated by an adversary who has a more relaxed mind and who understands that confidence is always lost through nervousness.

If we have playmind, we can see through meditation that all phenomena are like magic. Then, wherever we go, we are comfortable. If we come from a high standard class, we can do low standard work very easily without self-righteousness or discomfort. If we come from a low standard class, we can communicate easily with high standard people since our mind is vast and playful. Whatever class we come from, there is no contradiction between high and low standards because our mind is open and relaxed and we see all phenomena as the display of unobstructed Wisdom Mind.

If we have playmind, even if we speak with powerful leaders, we can speak just as powerfully as they do because our mind is free and fearless and we see all phenomena as the display of unobstructed Wisdom Mind.

If we have playmind, there is no contradiction between pure and impure, so whether or not we take religious vows, we automatically have pure morality, which depends on pure mind, free from negative conceptions. The purpose of vows is to transmute the impure to the pure. With playmind which is totally pure, we have no serious thought about breaking or keeping vows because we see all phenomena as the display of unobstructed Wisdom Mind.

If we have playmind, even if we leave our homeland, we can easily adapt to any custom because we are not serious about our own country's custom. With playmind we can adapt everywhere because we see all phenomena as the display of unobstructed Wisdom Mind.

When we practice, we need rested playmind. All spiritual qualities are invisible and substanceless and are inherent within all substance. If we are too serious, the aim of our meditation becomes more and more distant, because our mind is divided and obscured, but if we have playmind, our minds will always be clear, like the pond which becomes clear when left alone, free from disturbances.

Many teachers and texts say that we must be serious and diligent in our practice. But serious diligence does not mean only strict and narrow discipline. If we separate diligence from open space, it is the cause of ignorance. Real diligence is always the continuous energy of open playmind. Whenever we meditate, if we can leave our natural mind alone in playmind, our serious grasping mind cannot disturb us. We need a balanced mind between grasping too tightly and relaxing too loosely. When there is no more serious grasping mind, enlightenment is effortlessly close.

Once there was a discipline of Buddha Shakyamuni who could never rest his mind for even one moment between concentration that was too tight and concentration that was too loose. The Buddha asked him, "Before you became my disciple, did you ever play music?" The disciple answered, "Yes, I was an expert at playing the sitar." The Buddha asked, "Did a smooth sound come when the strings were tightly tuned?" and he said, "No." Again the Buddha asked, "Did a smooth sound come when the strings were loosely tuned?" And again he answered, "No." Then the Buddha said, "How did you get a smooth sound?" And he answered, "A smooth sound came when the sitar was tuned neither too tightly nor too loosely." The Buddha said, "Can you meditate the same way, with concentration that is neither too tight nor too loose?" When the disciple meditated with a balanced mind as the Buddha taught through the example of the sitar, he saw the nature of his Wisdom Mind.

If we are practicing visualization and have no expectation, then whatever kind of deity we visualize, we will spontaneously see Wisdom Deity. Too much serious concentration is the cause of grasping neurotic mind. If we try to visualize Wisdom Deity with serious squinting eyes and a grasping neurotic mind, our visualization becomes a demon since its source is dualistic mind. Where there is dualism, there is rejection and acceptance. Where there is rejection and acceptance, there is the cause of aversion and attachment. Where there is aversion and attachment, there is the cause of samsara.

So whatever our practice is, we need playmind, which is always unexpecting and vast. Playmind has no fear because it has no object. Because it is completely natural and open, it always gives bliss and blessing. If we have playmind, we can increase our natural wisdom energy. This light indestructible energy is very subtle and powerful, always a benefit to others since it is harmless and impenetrable by the gross element substance of others' energy. Because seriousness is an expression of the gross elements, the more serious something is the heavier it is and the more likely to become stuck in the heavy and divided from the light. The Buddha is totally light so we cannot say that he is serious. The Buddha is vast, pervading everywhere, and never divided.

In general, the students of the Hinayana system are taught to try to subdue the mind and abandon desirable qualities through discipline. But as Dharma practitioners, we usually grab only one word of the Buddha's teaching through this discipline. Really, the

Buddha's teaching is to benefit all sentient beings, and sentient beings always depend on desirable qualities. That is why the Buddha says you must offer all desirable qualities to the Triple Gems. This does not mean that the Buddha has five senses like we do to accept desirable qualities. The Buddha is only adapting to us so that we can play with desirable qualities and, through play, our mind can be released into its pure light energy.

The Buddha says that whoever understands magic compassion and whoever practices magic enlightenment is the best practitioner. Through magic, we can play using the secret potential of our elements. When we concentrate too seriously, then all elements gather together in serious conception, inner space becomes very congested and narrow, and where space is absent, there is darkness. In dark crowded space, there is no room for unobstructed mirror mind whose natural luminosity had been suppressed by serious mind. If there is no playmind luminosity, there can be no clear, discerning Wisdom Mind, which is the support and source of all qualities and phenomena.

Magic and the Mysterious

Snowflakes, though at a glance beautiful as flowers,
vanish when touched by the hand.

THE MINDS of all ordinary beings are magicians whose magic
is a deceptive trick through which truth is made untrue or
untruth is made true for pleasure or for suffering. People are afraid
of magic and become superstitious because they divide the gross
elements from the subtle elements and mistrust the connection
between them. This division habit results in an imbalance between
the gross and the subtle elements. Then, if a bad circumstance
arises such as an accident or sickness, we sometimes think it is
black magic coming from a magician, demon, or ghost. Of course
in general, until our dualistic mind is exhausted, we have negative
phenomena. Particular demons or ghosts do exist through these
phenomena, but we should never think they are different from
our own neurotic mind. We will always be fooled or tricked until
all black magicians have become transformed into white wisdom
magicians and until we have transformed our neurotic mind into
Wisdom Mind.

For ultimate benefit, the best antidote to use against magicians
is to dissolve all magic conceptions into great emptiness. Then by
watching our mind, the duality of the inner subject who sees the
magician and the outer object magician dissolves and becomes one
space Wisdom Mind. One space is always harmless because there
is no more harm-giving object and no more harm-receiving sub-

ject. All existent phenomena arise effortlessly in Wisdom Mind as unobstructed wisdom magic which always benefits and never harms.

But if we believe in magic, magicians, and demons, then for temporary benefit, it is necessary to have an antidote such as visualization as a defense to protect us. If we need protection against a magician whose energy element is predominantly fire, we can visualize either stronger fire elements or more powerful water elements. For protection against a demon whose energy element is predominantly water, we can use either stronger water elements or more powerful fire elements. If we need protection against violence caused by wrathfulness, the antidote is either more wrathful energy to conquer it or peaceful energy to subdue it. For protection against a magician who has ghost power, we can visualize powerful deities.

The essence of magic demons can be understood by examining their four different aspects. The obstruction demon appears as a result of our dependence on our obscured inner senses, which we use to create a link with the outer elements. For example, earthquakes, floods, and accidents are not inherently evil or good, and parents, family, friends, and lovers are not in themselves evil or good, yet when our ego links with these outer substance circumstances and interprets them, our conceptions becomes bad or good, or keep changing, and both bad and good interpretations become obstruction demons.

The unobstructed demon appears when feelings and moods arise which are not the result of outer substance circumstances and are not dependent on them. We are usually very concerned about these unobstructed demons because we cannot find a substance cause for our feelings and moods. In this generation, we often spend years with therapists in order to rid ourselves of these unobstructed demons, trying to explain and express them away.

The self-satisfaction demon of our worldly qualities appears when we interpret good circumstances such as position, friends, and comforts with pride and a sense of fulfillment and become attached to our good fortune. The self-satisfaction demon of our spiritual qualities is more subtle. For example, we may think our

spiritual path is superior, our teacher is best, our blissful or vision-
ary experiences are very special. Our mind becomes obscured by
self-importance with these thoughts and, because we cannot increase our pure qualities due to our obscured mind, we cannot
conquer the self-satisfaction demons.

The self-righteous demon appears when we interpret the self as
being better than the other with comparative concepts. For example, we may think, "I am more beautiful, more intelligent, more
gifted than they are."

In high Vajrayana Buddhism, deities are portrayed stamping on
four bodies. These bodies are symbolic of the annihilation of the
self-righteous demons.

> Lord Buddha, may I transform my ordinary body into
> splendid Wisdom Body, to be the same as you.
>
> Lord Buddha, may I conquer these four demons with your
> most wrathful aspect, to be the same as you.
>
> Lord Buddha, may I, with giant legs of strong compassion,
> crush and annihilate these four demons, to be the same
> as you.

Self-satisfaction demons and self-righteous demons are the most
dangerous for practitioners. Without realizing Wisdom Mind, a
practitioner may seem to become a saint or a sage without aban-
doning his ego, and through certain sadhanas, may attain great
powers like a magician. But without a true understanding of our
real wisdom nature and without confidence in our Wisdom Mind,
no matter what powers we attain through practice, if we cannot
release our mind from our ego's pride at having attained these
powers, it is only the cause of samsara.

Guru "Knowing Three Times" said, "There are so many saints,
but so few are realized." Without realizing Wisdom Mind, even
though a saint may be able to perform many great and varied miracles, if the essence of his magic is ego, he will only create self-
righteous and self-satisfaction demons which are great obstacles
to enlightenment. For this reason, the practitioner's path is very
difficult.

In general, until a scholar has complete confidence in his Wisdom Mind, he must practice secretly and alone. Many years ago, in India, there was a great scholar named Source of Teaching who lived and taught at the Buddhist university Nalanda. By practicing his deity's sadhana, he attained common siddhi, and was able to perform great miracles. While giving initiations, he could put ritual vessels in the sky without the support of his hands so that he could use his hands to make gestures. Although his mind was very powerful, his teacher instructed him not to leave Nalanda until he attained confidence in his Wisdom Mind. Nevertheless, he left the university with his one devoted student to perform the actions of a saint in the world.

On the road he met a girl who did not believe in Buddhism. Near a peach tree he asked her for some peaches but she said to him, "You take them yourself; I don't want to serve you." So he sat near the peach tree, and as he looked up, fruit fell in front of him like rain. Immediately the girl said, "Before you eat those peaches, look at me." As he looked at her, she looked down at the peaches and they all went back up into the tree, so he could not have even one peach. He became embarrassed and then angry. She told him, "Even though you are a very powerful yogi, you will see that after three nights you will not be alive."

He left with his student and after a while he became sick with blood in his urine. Even though he had deity's visualization power, his anxiety increased because his wisdom confidence was not great enough. He thought he was being punished by the deity for disobeying his teacher's advice not to leave the university until he had wisdom confidence.

He was told that his illness could only be cured by sea foam from the ocean. The ocean was far away, so he sent his student there to bring it to him. On the way back, the student met another girl on the road, who asked him where he was going in such a hurry. When he explained that his teacher was mortally sick, she replied sadly that he had already died. The student threw the sea foam away and ran to the town where he had left his teacher, but when he arrived he found him alive. His teacher asked, "Where is the sea foam?" and the student explained that the girl by the road had said he was dead. Then Source of Teaching knew he would die from the demon's power. Still, he decided to try through his own power to come back to his body after his death, and so he asked the student to protect his corpse.

When Source of Teaching died, this same girl, who was a witch, emanated many wolves who circled around his house during the night, scratching at neighbors' doors and howling loudly so that the whole town knew there was a corpse nearby. During the day she appeared and spread news about where the corpse could be found, so the townspeople came and took the body away to burn it. After three days had passed, a whirlwind appeared near the student, and from it a voice spoke, saying, "In this life I could not become enlightened, but maybe I will be able to in the bardo."

Many Buddhist texts mention other examples of obstacles created by self-righteous and self-satisfaction demons. Practitioners like Source of Teaching may have been emanated by the Buddha to teach us how to recognize the effects of these demons. If we are intelligent or famous for our intellect but lack wisdom confidence, we must always guard against self-righteous demons and self-satisfaction demons in order to practice in a pure way. Without complete confidence in our Wisdom Mind, we will continue to be deceived by magic, whether we think it is the magic of demons or whether we think it is the magic of our own neurotic minds. Without really understanding, we will view anything mysterious with suspicion, separating subject from object, subtle from gross, and mistrusting the real nature of the wisdom mystery inherent in our own minds.

Whatever we cannot explain we say is mysterious because its subtle elements' expression is hidden within gross elements. All hidden qualities are mysterious. We can say that tomorrow is mysterious, next year is mysterious, the future is mysterious, because they are inconspicuous and have not yet occurred. We never think that daytime phenomena are mysterious because they are conspicuous and gross, but we think that dream phenomena are mysterious because they are inconspicuous and subtle. We think what is hidden is unreliable and reject what we feel is mysterious, but in fact since neither is permanent, both daytime phenomena and dreamtime phenomena are unreliable. When we dream, our waking phenomena are inconspicuous. When we wake, our dream phenomena are inconspicuous. Each is equally mysterious and magical from the point of view of the other.

We often think that because dreamtime is short it is not true, while because daytime is long it is true. But sometimes in a dream we can complete a long task in one instant which we never could finish in ordinary daytime and we can travel long distances within a moment which in daytime might take many days. Whether short or long, dreamtime and daytime are only created magically by conception and actually neither is true. Both are equally unreliable, impermanent, and mysterious.

Many nonreligious people distrust religions in general, and particularly Buddhism, because they seem mysterious. But still they trust and accept many mysterious worldly situations. Smugglers, for instance, are mysterious to customs officials. Because they believe in the mysteriousness of smugglers, customs officials are suspicious of everyone, including nonsmugglers. Automatically they believe the mysterious is everywhere; this is their job. Smugglers are suspicious of all customs officials, whether or not they are actually going to check them. Without believing in the mysteriousness of the customs official, how can a smuggler remain hidden and protect his own mysteriousness? As a result, all the time, wherever they are, smugglers and customs officials are mutually engaged in suspecting and expressing the mysterious as if it were their religion.

The explainable is always inherent in the unexplainable mysterious, and the unexplainable mysterious is always inherent in the explainable. Smugglers have customs officials inherent within them, and customs officials have smugglers inherent within them. What is inherent manifests through suspicion, and they try to fool each other from one's mysteriousness to another's mysteriousness.

Everywhere in samsara, governments believe in the mysterious without recognizing it. A country which has mysterious power can often conquer a country whose power is conspicuous. Some governments have organizations such as the KGB and CIA which are based on secrecy. These organizations are mysterious to each other and everyone else. Because their power comes from the mysterious, when their secrets become conspicuous they are always replaced by other secrets. As a result, other countries' organizations can never understand what they are going to do or how to deal with them.

Our ego's self-protecting paranoia creates suspicion, and this suspicion is the source of samsara's mysteriousness, which is the cause of more suspicion. We are always suspicious that outer objects will harm us, and so we create separation and division. But we are never suspicious that these same objects are the Buddha, our own mysterious mind, never separate from us, and the source of nirvana's mysteriousness.

If people can believe in samsara's mystery, then they should also be able to believe in nirvana's mystery. We can say that sentient beings are mysterious because, through lack of wisdom confidence, they are fooled by their own unreliable phenomena, and the unreliable is always mysterious. We can also say that the Buddha is mysterious because his sublime qualities are hidden from us because of our obscured minds.

Samsara's mysteriousness created by dualistic mind always causes us to be fooled. We cannot abandon samsara's mysteriousness unless we believe in nirvana's mysteriousness. If we reject nirvana's mysteriousness, it causes ignorance, while if we believe in it, we cannot be fooled by the objects of dualistic phenomena.

Samsara's mysteriousness created by dualistic mind is always the cause of suffering, while nirvana's mysteriousness protects and releases us from suffering. Samsara's mysteriousness is an endless circle of the unexplainable turning into the explainable and back again into the unexplainable over and over, again and again. This is because samsara's mysteriousness always exists with time and between subject and object. Because we have expectations towards objects, when we lose them our subject mind suffers and creates new objects. In this way we are bound to opposites, such as existence and nonexistence, and we believe in opposites as necessary. When we are thinking of our upper body, our lower body becomes mysterious. When we think of front, back is mysterious. Front and back depend on one another according to dualistic mysteriousness; you cannot have one without the other, but you can only have one at a time. Likewise, what we see may be male, but the mysterious female is always inherent, revealed through the subtle elements existing within the gross. The mysterious is hidden; it is necessary but unexpressed, or expressed subtly. If we do not believe in opposites, we are open to enlightenment's mystery.

Mysterious sublime qualities are always beneficial. They cause mind to become less and less dependent on objects, allowing the unexplainable and explainable to join together inseparably. Sublime people no longer depend on subject and object or time and place and cannot be fooled by samsara's mysterious phenomena. But ordinary-minded people cannot catch hidden sublime qualities, and so these qualities seem threatening and mysterious. What is unknown is always mysterious, so if we do not know our mind, it is always mysterious. Because our mind is the ultimate mystery, Dharma, which is the expression of our mind's pure qualities, must also be mysterious. Because our mind is mysterious, ordinary external phenomena which come from mind are also mysterious.

According to samsara's ordinary substance mysteriousness, water is more mysterious than earth because it is lighter, more unstable, and moving. Fire is more mysterious than water because it is lighter, faster, and less touchable. Air is more mysterious than fire because it is still lighter and more invisible. But space is the most mysterious of all because it is never dull, never empty, most invisible, and most open. If there were no space, there could be no earth, no water, no fire and no air. Space pervades all the elements.

The ordinary mysterious has an impure aspect and a pure aspect. Mysteriousness is impure when our mind's pure phenomena change to impure phenomena, as, for instance, when the deity we visualize becomes a demon through our own impure phenomena. Mysteriousness is pure when our mind's impure phenomena change to pure phenomena, for instance, when we transform a demon into Wisdom Deity. If we grasp at deity phenomena in our visualization without recognizing Wisdom Deity, these phenomena become impure. But if we understand how to visualize through wisdom phenomena, we can transform demon's obstructed phenomena into deity's pure unobstructed phenomena.

Magic and the Mysterious

The Buddha's Wisdom Mind is pure and mysterious. It protects us because it is ultimately uncatchable and secret and so cannot be penetrated by the temporary worldly mysterious. The Buddha's Wisdom Mind is unobstructed and always benefits everyone without intention through pure mysterious wisdom energy which pervades all the elements and is always free. The Buddha's Wisdom Mind has mysterious wisdom power which never ends, is never stuck anywhere, and is never affected by samsara's obstructed explainable phenomena. If we can recognize our own mysterious secret wisdom essence, which is the same from the beginning as Buddha's mysterious secret wisdom essence, then enlightenment is no longer mysterious to us because, inseparable from the Buddha, we are the mysterious.

> The earthquake cannot harm the mysterious sky no matter how much its powerful shaking overturns and destroys.
> The ocean cannot harm the mysterious sky no matter how much its turbulent waves flood and destroy.
> The fire cannot harm the mysterious sky no matter how much its angry flames burn and destroy.
> The hurricane cannot harm the mysterious sky no matter how much its violent winds blow and destroy.

Healing

A stone patch on wood will not fit suitably.

A CCORDING TO Wisdom Mind, the elements of phenomena are unobstructed and pure. Pure phenomena are natural, unobscured, and uncontrived by gross elements. They are light, invisible, impenetrable, insubstantial, and indestructible because nothing remains inertly anywhere. Where nothing remains, nothing can be diminished or enhanced. Where nothing can be diminished or enhanced, there is balance and purity. Where there is balance and purity, there is health.

According to ordinary dualistic mind, the elements of phenomena are obstructed and impure. Impure phenomena are obscured and contrived by the gross elements: They are heavy, visible, penetrable, substantial, and destructible because they remain inertly somewhere. Where something remains, it can be diminished or enhanced. Where it can be diminished or enhanced, there is imbalance and impurity. Where there is imbalance and impurity, there is sickness.

The five elements appear less and less subtle as they take on the qualities attributed to them by ordinary mind. If a doctor does not believe in the invisible pure essence of the elements, his diagnosis may be wrong, as he can only treat sickness through visible and impure elements. Even so, the more experienced a doctor is, the subtler his point of view and diagnosis will be. He may treat obvious outer symptoms to obtain immediate specific visible results which are only temporary, or he may treat subtler inner symptoms to obtain less visible, more balanced, and more gradual benefits. These, while still temporary, come closer to the invisible source of the illness. But however subtle his treatment may be, if he perceives phenomena as separate from their pure essence, his ability to help will be limited.

The experienced doctor realizes that basically all the elements are mutually dependent. Because each of the elements has the other four inherently within it and combinations of the elements vary and constantly change according to karma, the temperaments and health of people are also constantly changing. As a result, proper medical treatment deals with illness by correcting imbalances in the elements from the subtlest point of view. To accomplish this, the five elements are combined into many different categories of treatment according to many different systems of medicine.

Because the elements are mutually dependent, they can be considered divided only in their specific applications for specific effects. The effectiveness of these divisions depends on the doctor's ability to recognize which impure elements in a patient are diminished and need to be increased, or which are too abundant and need to be decreased, and how to apply the treatment so that it will reach the subtlest levels in order to restore balance.

In this way, it is sometimes appropriate to use an element to enhance itself, as fire with fire when the patient's subtler heat elements have diminished. At other times, one element is used to neutralize another, as fire with water when the patient's subtler heat elements have increased. A person with a fire element fever can be treated with grains or herbs that are grown in a cool climate; a person with a water element chill can be treated with grains or herbs that are grown in a warm climate.

The compatibility and effects of elements often depend on the subtlety of their applications. For instance, fire is not always the enemy of water. When water is heated by fire, vapor may result, which is lighter and purer than the original water and cooler than the original fire. For certain imbalances, this subtler vapor may be more appropriate than either element used separately. In the same way, the positive or negative effects of the elements depend on the subtlety of their use. Some medicines taken in large amounts become poisons; some poisons taken in small doses become medicines. Too much medicine for fever can give chills; too much insulin for diabetes can cause shock. Sometimes two poisons combine to form another poison, and sometimes they form a medicine, but the positive and negative qualities of the elements used in treatment must always be balanced.

The potential of ordinary mind to understand the pure elements varies according to karma, so conceptions of pure and impure will differ from one being to another. Many flies and insects are attracted to pus, while intelligent human beings think of pus as infected water. Human beings believe blood is purer than pus. Experienced practitioners recognize that the inner source element of both pus and blood is water, which becomes healing wisdom nectar through the pure perception of their practice.

The ordinary doctor who does not understand that the invisible essence of the elements is inherent within the substance elements does not know how to balance and purify the impure elements. Because of this, he cannot treat a diminishing or increasing element properly and may harm other elements by prescribing the wrong treatment. For instance, when a person with a rare blood type is sick, an ordinary doctor may only recommend a transfusion and try to find the specific blood type for the exchange of substance blood. He expects an immediate visible reaction rather than the slower process of locating the water elements suitable for restoring the balance of the gross elements through an understanding of the pure essence of blood.

But whether blood is increased through natural foods or medicines which contain the water element, or through a blood transfusion which contains the water element, if the doctor is a nihilist and only believes in substance, then when the visible elements of his treatment are exhausted, or when the suitable blood type for the transfusion is not available, his power to help is also exhausted and the disease returns. The patient's gross elements then become weakened through anxiety, so that he can no longer be helped. But if the doctor understands and believes in the invisible wisdom

essence of the elements, he can help his patient with subtle methods and comfort him through this belief so that the natural balance
of the patient's elements can be restored and his sickness can be
healed.

The elements pervade all phenomena, and because mind pervades all the elements, if a doctor tells a patient that he has a can-
cerous tumor, the patient may focus with fear on the tumor,
making it grow larger. This focus originates from the subtle fire
element of his anxiety, which increases the growth of the disease
by its destructive burning aspect. If the doctor can understand the
invisible elements, he can restore the natural balance of the elements in his patient's mind through the natural balance of the elements in his own understanding mind. He can then comfort and
encourage him to focus positively, dissolving the tumor through
visualization and meditation. Even if through karma the patient
dies, this positive focus is a benefit for him because he will not
have any cancer residue or seed of new cancer in his afterlife or
rebirth.

According to the Tantric system, the root circumstances of birth
are created by karmic links; the contributing circumstances are the
father's sperm and the mother's egg. Rebirth occurs when these
come together in the absence of impure air. Through the energy
of karmic air, the sperm and egg unite, forming the embryo. The
energy of the body manifests from the energy of the karmic air,
originating in and increasing from the navel center of the embryo.
Through this energy, the embryo becomes elongated. Then the
subtle energy of the whole body condenses from the navel source
to form nerves and veins. Finally, the central life channels extend
from the throat chakra to form the head chakra of great exaltation.
In all, the body's form develops and grows in the womb for ap-
proximately thirty-eight weeks through the energy of karmic air.

The increase of bones, marrow, and brains comes predominantly from the influence of the father's sperm, while the increase
of flesh and blood comes predominantly from the influence of the
mother's egg. The solid part of the body, such as flesh and bones,
comes predominantly from the qualities of the earth element, and
as they increase they give birth to the nose and the sense of smell.

The liquid parts of the body, such as the blood, come predominantly from the qualities of the water element, and as they increase they give birth to the tongue and the sense of taste. The heat and complexion of the body come predominantly from the qualities of the fire element, and as they increase they give birth to the eyes and the sense of sight. The breathing of the body comes predominantly from the qualities of the air element, and as they increase they give birth to sensation throughout the body and the sense of touch. The spaces connecting outer and inner elements which are the support of life come predominantly from the qualities of the space element, and as they increase they give birth to the ears and the sense of hearing.

Without the earth element, there is no basis for support; without the water element, there is no basis for gathering and collecting; without the fire element, there is no basis for ripening; without the air element, there is no basis for increasing; without the space element, there is no door to expansion. Thus, all root and contributing circumstances combine to result in birth.

A child born with balanced elements will be born with a balanced mind. If the elements are not balanced at birth, it may result in a hysterical mind. Imbalances may be caused by uncomplementary elements within the contributing circumstances of the father's sperm and mother's egg. However, sometimes children of complementary parents are born with hysterical energy. In this case, the real source of hysteria is not the parents' physical bodies in this life but the subtle invisible elements of the children's root circumstance karmic energy from previous lives.

In general, imbalances among the elements resulting in hysteria may be caused by many different external circumstances, such as family, business, fame, power, Dharma, and politics. These outer circumstances are the source of too much depression and elation, which in turn cause frustration, fragility, and disappointment. Whenever the mind's inner personal elements depend on outer general elements, the mind becomes weak and easily affected by them. When the external circumstances appear temporarily bad, causing excessive depression, the mind's inner elements become agitated and lose their strength. This agitation causes instability of

the inner elements, leaving the mind fragile like the blue flame of
a flickering oil lamp whose fuel is almost spent. In this condition,
the mind cannot expand among the balanced elements of equanimity. When external circumstances appear temporarily good,
causing excessive elation, the mind's inner elements become agitated and overwhelmingly strong, causing the mind's energy to
rise out of control like water under pressure shooting out of an
uncapped pipe. All the channels in the body are flooded, and energy cannot be composed within the balanced elements of equanimity.

More specifically, hysteria can be caused when rigid parents or
teachers with strict traditions, who really do not understand the
light quality of children's energy, control and calculate according
to the elements of their own heavy, mature energy. Since the con-
tainer of the children's minds cannot absorb all these different energy elements, they become frustrated and fearful, and between
fears and frustration the seed of hysteria is planted. When these
children grow up, they have residual frustrations and fears and become hysterical through this stressed mind. Pleasant distraction is
the antidote to this type of hysteria.

When the elements of two people are uncomplementary and
their minds do not suit each other, it may result in hysteria. According to the nihilist point of view, men and women come together as a result of coincidence. According to the Buddhist point
of view, men and women come together as a result of ripening
karma dormant within their inner elements, joining in love when
all the individual subtle and gross elements complement each
other. When they unite in sex and their subtle elements are complementary, they create gross complementary elements, culminat-
ing in orgasms. If their subtle elements are compatible, they can
benefit each other by linking externally through the gross elements, which enables their lighter inner elements to also link. But
if their elements become incompatible by changing, diminishing,
or contradicting each other, there is no longer any life connection
or comforting between them, and this can create hysteria.

Hysteria is also caused by too much reaching and grasping in all
directions towards all objects and knowledge. Since all substance

is impermanent, while one object is reached, another is lost, and between reaching and missing, the mind's energy is never composed within the heart. This type of hysterical mind is scattered everywhere, always trying to reach something. Because constant involvement with external phenomena causes turbulence, it is sometimes a benefit for this kind of person to be in dark, silent, quiet places, abstaining from talk, music, and song. Parents, teachers, or doctors who want to help with skillful means should try to balance and compose their inner energy without force.

Another cause of hysteria is competition. There are so many countless scientists, philosophers, scholars, artists, and others whose ultimate intention is to invent something new. Because they are racing to make the best invention, there is constant competition and the stress of this competition causes hysteria. The antidote for this is also to try to balance and compose inner energies without force.

Hysteria may also be caused by striving after subtle substance. As scientists, philosophers, scholars, artists, or meditators, if we do not use our pure elements with wisdom practice, we may find that we use our minds in a subtle intellectual way, going deeper and deeper, seeking the finest, most subtle elements in substance. But through this ordinary aim, we become trapped in fine substance and our mind can never find space to go beyond into the substanceless. When we are not aware of the pure essence of the elements and we have no space in which to relax, our inner subtle elements become congested, losing their power and frustrating us. Then, like outer element air which has become turbulent from the heat of the sun, causing clouds to gather and rain to fall, we internalize and suppress our emotions, condensing the subtle inner elements of our life force, which become crowded, constantly colliding among themselves, moving turbulently and hysterically, connecting with the body's outer elements at the heart, and creating heart water and explosive hysterical expressions.

Whatever its source, subtle element turbulence will cause our inner gross element nerves, veins, and breathing to become unstable, forcing us to depend on our outer gross elements. These outer gross elements have the power to delude us when our mind's inner subtle elements become weakened, as the sun's fire element has the power to make us hallucinate if our subtle elements are not strong enough. Then the turbulent energy of our body's action and speech becomes as hysterical as our mind. Since it is more congested and under pressure, the turbulent energy of hysterics is stronger than other people's. As a result they can create and destroy many things, and can hurt or benefit depending on whether they are among uncomplementary or complementary elements.

An external sign of hysteria is constant nervous movement. This can result in harmful accidents. When we reach for a cup, it breaks; when we cook, we burn or cut ourselves; when we walk, we fall; when we are with people, we become sad easily; when we talk, we blurt; when we lie down, we cannot sleep; when we sleep, we have turbulent and threatening dreams; when we think, before one thought has ended another begins.

Hysteria can also produce specific external illnesses because conceptions are inseparable from karmic air which contains all the elements. Those who are nervous, who do not have a resting mind, have continuous moving conceptions. This persistent activity generates conspicuous warmth which is the essence of the fire element. Fire and air are connected to each other through their similar subtle qualities. To ordinary mind, the subtle fire element is more conspicuous and substantial than the subtle air element. This combination of air and fire causes the elements to manifest in increasingly gross form, mixing with the water and earth elements. For example, if through karma, the five elements are not well balanced in the body, and the earth and water elements in one of the body's organs have diminished, then the fire and air elements become agitated by the mind's hysterical conceptions, and the irritation of the gross elements by the fiery movement of the mind within the karmic air may result in sicknesses like sores, ulcers, and cancer.

As long as our ordinary mind remains obscured and imbalanced, we will continue to become hysterical through our impure element conceptions. Because our ordinary mind constantly needs an object, we never acknowledge that Wisdom Mind goes beyond conceptions. We are obscured by this ignorance, which is related to the heavy earth element. Then we want to know something about these conceptions; this desire is related to the water element. Then, because we do not have a wisdom point of view, we cannot find anything and become angry, frustrated, and jealous, not knowing where to rest. This anger and pride are related to the fire and air elements.

If we are hysterical, we cannot find the vast pure secret essence of the elements no matter how often or constantly we try. We become more and more divided and stuck where there is no space, no rest, and no more belief in vast space beyond conception. Because subtle and gross elements depend constantly on each other, we are reborn into these same turbulent gross element bodies with the same hysterical subtle element minds. When our previous lives' hysterical circumstances, created predominantly by fire and air elements through negative phenomena, connect in our next life with new negative phenomena, we become more hysterical with more fiery anger and airy frustration. When our previous lives' hysterical circumstances, created predominantly by fire and air elements through negative phenomena, connect in our next life with new positive phenomena, we become more hysterical with more watery elation.

Water, like fire, is sometimes positive and sometimes negative. In order to be helped, the hysterical person must be separated from his positive, overly elated mind or his negative, overly depressed mind until he attains a natural balanced mind. The elements causing this elation or depression must be found. Whether it is from the water element desire or the fire element anger, the treatment depends on the particular circumstances of the individual. For example, if the fire element is conspicuous in a patient, the psychologist with experience can create a conspicuous water element as an antidote. If the patient is angry, he can create a calm atmosphere to soothe the patient. If the patient is hiding a problem behind a calm surface, the doctor can create a fiery atmosphere to bring out his real anger. Through understanding the patient's expression of his elements, the psychologist can transform them to create the necessary balance. If he cannot understand the nature of the elements which are contained within the expression of his patient's mood, he is only like a babysitter, giving his patient toys to temporarily pacify him.

Experienced doctors understand that the best way to balance the elements is through appropriate subtle medicines, such as visualization, yoga breathing exercises, and meditation. Meditation, or watching the mind, is especially effective for diminishing pain and curing sickness. Through watching, the basis for pain and sickness dissolves because pain and sickness are conception and are within the gross elements. Through this watching, gross elements dissolve into subtle elements, and subtle elements become lighter and lighter until there is only clear space and the five elements pervade inconspicuously and inseparably beyond any conception of sickness or pain. Then, selfless clear space mind, balanced from the beginning, is free from all distinction between pure and impure elements.

Energy and Power

An intelligent person can benefit from others
without hurting them
as a bee can sip nectar from
a flower without harming it.

From the beginning the subtle and gross energy of our elements is inseparable from emptiness. When we express ourselves excessively with excitement, we exaggerate our gross element energy and depress our subtle element energy. As a result, our energy is directed predominantly towards substance and its natural connection to emptiness is obscured. Because substance is impermanent, when new circumstances arise and the substance object of our excited energy changes or is lost, our energy is also lost and we feel anxious and depressed. In this way, our energy is like a river and has a natural flow. If a river's energy is excessive, it will flood. Afterwards when its flood energy has been exhausted, a ruin is left behind. If we let our gross energy flood, we get tired easily because our mind loses its subtle energy support. If through skillful means we are able to conserve subtle energy by expressing it carefully in small amounts with pauses, then it is temporarily good for our health and mood, whether we are alone or with people, and eventually a benefit to us as we get older.

Sometimes we are afraid our energy's power will be wasted if we do not use it immediately as the opportunity presents itself. But problems may arise if the mind's form is expressed immediately in reaction to circumstances. Power expressed without foresight always returns eventually, reversing confidence into pathetic impotence. Some of us think that gross power is most effective when expressed visibly rather than with invisible equanimity. But when we can only see in front of us and cannot provide for the future, this is only ignorance. If a wild lion tries to kill the bear in front of him while unaware of the hunter trying to kill him from behind, he loses his power.

According to worldly custom, when we make plans for business or try to organize our life, it is best to keep energy contained without expressing it until we get results. According to Dharma custom, it is also best to keep our energy contained until we develop confidence. That way even if the result does not come immediately, our energy will not be dissipated and exhausted.

People cannot see each other's invisible mind until circumstances arise. Then the mind's form becomes conspicuous through expression and can be engaged and contacted. Even before this happens, certain kinds of demons or spirits and ghosts can perceive it. But by keeping our energy contained with strong and relaxed mind, we can protect and benefit ourselves. Spiritual and sublime beings with transparent mind can also perceive what has not yet been expressed, but naturally, since they have Wisdom Mind, they only benefit us.

To the extent that it is powerful, the energy inherent in our elements supports our mind. In order to increase our energy's power, we must have a method with an aim. Where there is an aim, there is energy. Where there is energy, there is power. For instance, when we want to be warm, if we concentrate toward the fire element, we can become warm. When we want to be cool, if we concentrate towards the water and air elements, we can become cool. This is because by concentrating we can make different subtle elements become more conspicuous with substance power. If we aim with substance means, it is always impermanent because aim is part of conception, which is impermanent. If our goal is only to gain worldly power for our temporary benefit rather than to become enlightened, no matter where we aim with our subtle and gross elements, we can only attain our goal for a limited time in a limited way.

People can increase their energy's power with either bad or good intention. If their intention is bad, they can harm other beings by conquering them to increase their own power. But by using their outer elements' energy, they will succeed only until their inner elements' energy, accumulated over many lives, is diminished or exhausted. Some world leaders have caused great destruction and suffering through their energy's power and their bad intentions. Other world leaders, like Mahatma Gandhi, benefitted people with their pure elements' energy. Those who want to help and comfort others through their good intention can develop the pure energy of great compassion and take rebirth as Bodhisattvas.

Sometimes our mind's pure element energy can be disturbed from afar by a mind whose energy is impure. For example, if we are expecting a guest whose elements are more polluted and more powerful than our own, his mind's energy may enter into ours and disturb our sleep. Because our mind's energy is more pure and sensitive than his, the imbalance between his elements and ours may cause a disruption in our habitual pattern of sleep and we may dream about the guest or have insomnia. If the guest's mind is as pure as our own, it is unlikely that our mind will be disturbed, but if our elements' energy is less powerful than his, we must depend on an antidote to increase our power. When our pure elements' energy has more power than his impure elements' energy, he cannot disturb our mind, and so we do not need an antidote to sleep. We are able to rest in our balanced mind and ultimately we can be a benefit to him.

According to worldly custom, food and medicines are the antidote for light sleep which is caused by light mind. They give us heavy foggy mind, which causes heavy sleep. But if we really want to increase our pure energy's power, we can visualize deity, which will strengthen our mind so that an ordinary powerful mind cannot penetrate it. If we practice meditation, we can inhale all of the elements so that our inner and outer elements are mixed inseparably and our mind pervades everywhere, dissolving into clear space. By making our mind lighter and clearer through visualization or meditation, we may gain such powers as clairvoyance and precognition, but if we become too attached to these powers, our energy loses its mobility. So continuously, without acceptance or rejection, we should just use and increase this pure energy.

There are countless different types of power, but they all can be divided into two different categories: ordinary intellectual power and noble intelligent power. If we have ordinary narrow minds, it is appropriate for others to use heavy impure elements' intellectual power with us because we cannot understand the deep, clear, and vast. It is hopeless if people use subtle pure elements' intelligent power directly with us, because our containers are too small to hold it. With our ordinary narrow minds we cannot imagine the deep meaning, distant view, or what will happen in the future because our target is limited to the temporary and immediate benefit of ourselves at the expense of others. This is like slaughtering the cow who supplies daily milk just to eat one meal.

Noble, intelligent people do not use or accept ordinary intellectual power because it is too small and too narrow, too shallow and too rigid, too one-sided and too fixed in time for them. If we accept ordinary power, our minds cannot be vast. Without a vast mind there can be no great power, and only with great power can we adapt to the many different faculties among individual beings and act in time, go in time, release in time, help in time, and develop in time.

People who do not have noble intelligent power often use worldly politics in spiritual groups. Because those who want to study or learn generally depend on tradition, social customs, or politics, Dharma institutions cannot be made without some form of dependence on these. But, if we really want to make pure Dharma institutions, we must only temporarily depend on the heavy elements of society's customs in order to ultimately go beyond into wisdom's customless light elements. If we only believe in using our ordinary gross impure elements' power to help ourselves, we will automatically make hierarchies to prevent others in a gross or subtle way from being equal. Then those who desire inwardly to lift themselves up to a pure lighter level will be forced to use external power, depending on worldly institutions for advancement. Finally, as a result of this kind of ordinary hierarchical style in which those on top try to keep others down, everyone's mind becomes heavy.

People with ordinary minds who try to catch the minds of those of a higher level have respectful intention, not evolutionary intention. If our mind's intention can connect with natural, pure, vast luminosity power by outwardly depending on social custom while inwardly depending on the pure light essence of the elements, we can create purer and greater energy. Even if we only use ordinary intellectual power, when we meet with people who use pure noble intelligent power, we automatically get a sense of expansiveness rather than one of rejection or confinement to a lower level. In this way, some pure and gifted meditators create a field of bliss around themselves through their spontaneous luminous power, and use their pure elements to help others attain the same level and join with them in the same mandala and same mind.

Respect

I bow and pay homage
to secret stainless all-noble wisdom land.

THE ESSENCE of all manners and politeness is respect. In ancient times when pure inner qualities were naturally respected and considered most noble, people became kings, queens, and aristocrats through their pure essence politeness and manners. Their natural integrity was respected by people with pure minds, so they held this pure custom lineage for many generations, no matter how their circumstances changed.

Our natural nobility essence is pure from the beginning, but in modern times our inner elements have become obstructed and are not subtly refined, so we can no longer connect with our natural nobility lineage. Instead we attach to impermanent gross circumstances, and when these circumstances change, our behavior often becomes gross, arrogant, and fickle. True nobility is like gold, which is always unchanged by circumstances. Even if you burn it, it is still gold; even if you cut it, it is still gold; even if you grind it, it is still gold.

Whether we are born into aristocracy or try to become noble through wealth, power, and prestige, we cannot have pure unchanging inner nobility habits unless we have accumulated them from previous karma. If we do not have the habit of deeply respecting the pure unchanging essence of society's manners but only superficially adapt to their impermanent gross expression, we misuse our power and position through this shortsightedness and are only unreliable, artificial aristocrats.

These days, people from substance poor countries often have contempt for nobility because they mistakenly associate true noble essence with false aristocracy's gross impure actions. People from substance power countries cannot recognize true noble qualities because, through technology's machine habit mind, they have become too impatient to learn respect. But people from all countries try to find noble qualities such as honesty, kindness, courage, and generosity when choosing their leaders, because they understand that respect creates harmony and understanding among beings.

If we rely on impure gross elements and inert substance, our external power may increase while our pure inner elements diminish; then true respect is lost and there is disharmony and violence. When we have material habits, we only respect what we can use while we are using it. If we see sublime people, we may only respect them temporarily, but not deeply and unchangeably from our hearts. We cannot appreciate or benefit from their spiritual qualities because we see them from a substance point of view for our own entertainment. Our minds become more and more stuck in the artificial and inert objects of our concern, so we are unable to connect with their true essence. But if our aim is enlightenment, we must respect sublime people with spiritual qualities and depend on them to sharpen our faculties.

From the worldly point of view, the true purpose of respect is to show that culture and tradition are precious and to become knowledgeable and venerable by recognizing their precious qualities. From the Dharma point of view, the true purpose of respect is to connect mind to mind through pure inner substanceless qualities in order to develop pure outer substance qualities which again create more pure inner substanceless qualities.

There are many kinds of respect within the expressions of body, speech, and mind, but if the source of respect is not our mind, then the expression of our respect is false. That is why Buddha Shakyamuni said, "All existent phenomena are naturally in mind. Mind is primary and exists before the actions of body and speech.

Whoever speaks and acts with pure mind is always happy, just as shadows never separate from their source."

Many teachers say that we can only respect Dharma with our mind if we also respect it with our body and speech, but there are people who respect Dharma with their body and speech and are still disrespectful with their mind. For instance, when our teacher is in the shrine room and we kneel before the altar, but we stretch out our legs as soon as he leaves us alone, this is disrespect. When we address our teacher as Master or Your Holiness but then speak of him to others using a nickname, this is disrespect. These two expressions of body and speech show the disrespect of our impure mind. Where there is artificial respect, there is no real politeness and no pure nobility.

To show true respect in a consistently deep and subtle way we must make our minds pure. Then our respect will not be two-faced. It is always best to examine our mind before automatically saying that we respect someone, remembering that true respect always comes from the mind. If traditional outer rules of respect for body and speech are taught rigidly, without skillful means, we become fearful that we will disobey or betray the tradition. When our minds are fearful, our pure light inner elements become congested, and we can react by becoming wild, rebellious, and disrespectful. If we learn the inner respect of good intention, which exists within the pure light essence of the elements, then the outer expression of our body and speech will be open, pure, and unobstructed, and our respect will always be continuous.

One person's respect is another person's disrespect, and one person's disrespect is another person's respect. Some people's modest disciplined style is disrespectful to the conceited open-minded style of other people. Sometimes the open-minded conceited style of some people is disrespectful to the modest disciplined style of other people.

Since intimacy comes from love and trust, if we hide and distance ourselves from intimate friends, using strangers' formal expressions of respect with them, this is disrespectful to intimacy's respect. If we use private intimate expressions of respect with strangers in public, this is disrespectful to formality's respect. Expressions which are not disrespectful in private may be disrespectful in a group. For example, if through our privacy habit, we lie down and fart among a group of strangers, then this is inappropriate and disrespectful.

If we often use slang, it can be disrespectful to the literary style of scholars and philosophers; if we use verbose, complicated language, it can be disrespectful to the unobstructed mirrorlike natural language of the saints. If we write countless explanations analytically and elaborately and cannot synthesize them into their essence, it is disrespectful to the style of scholars, philosophers, and saints.

When someone is giving advice with good intention, it is disrespectful not to reply, "I understand." Even if we already know what they are trying to tell us, it is disrespectful to say, "I know that" instead of "Thank you." If we use satire and sarcasm with the intention of benefitting others, it may seem like disrespect to some, but it is really respect. If we use sweet speech and politeness to flatter others with the intention of benefitting ourselves, even though outwardly this may seem like respect, inwardly it is really a disrespectful trick.

If we teach Dharma to people who do not have the capacity or desire to understand it, this is disrespectful to Dharma. If we teach Dharma to people who already understand it, this is disrespectful to those we try to teach.

The respect for practice of some wandering gypsy students looks like disrespect to some restrained practitioners. The respect for Dharma of some restrained monks on retreat looks like disrespect to some scholars of religion or philosophy who think the monk is not really doing anything. Some people on retreat respect the retreat, but have no respect for human beings or animals. Respect and disrespect always depend on the pure intention of the inner elements.

If we are monks and do not have natural moral mind or weariness of samsara, yet we try to keep our vows externally with the expression of the certain action of body and speech in order to gain people's respect, we become military academy monks, which is disrespectful to pure monks.

Respect

If we do not recognize our own inner light Wisdom Dakini and only respect outer gross phenomena dakinis while justifying ourselves through the Tantric system, then we become aphrodisiac yogis, which is disrespectful to the pure yogi.

If we do not practice Dharma but only talk continuously without faith in our teacher, his teachings, his empowerments, our practice, and our retreats, making a Dharma shopping list, then our impure minds become constipated and we get dharmarhoids, which is disrespectful to the true Dharma practitioner and to pure Dharma.

If we do not believe in peaceful nirvana through aversion to samsara, then this is disrespectful to the Hinayana teaching. Even if we believe in the one extreme of peaceful nirvana through aversion to the other extreme of the suffering of samsara, this is still disrespectful to the Mahayana teachings because we then abandon all sentient beings in samsara in order to always remain in nirvana for our own self-benefit. Even though we may have respect for the Hinayana and Mahayana systems, if we do not have skillful means to swiftly transform samsara's conditions into Wisdom Deity, this is disrespectful to the Vajrayana system.

Whoever prays to female deities such as Tara is disrespectful to the Hinayana system. Whoever discriminates between all sentient beings, whether male or female, from insects to humans, without acknowledging their inherent Buddha-nature, is disrespectful to the Mahayana system. Whoever does not accept that Wisdom Deity is beyond our ordinary mind and does not make pure offerings is disrespectful to the Outer Tantric system. Whoever does not understand that the pure nature of the mind is free from mental activity, and does not establish that their mind is great emptiness, is disrespectful to the Madhyamika teaching. Whoever does not understand the pure nature of samsara's and nirvana's phenomena and cannot recognize that wisdom gesture pervades everywhere is disrespectful to Mahamudra's teaching.

Whoever sees that there is no difference between a seed, which contains all the elements dormantly, and its result is disrespectful to the ordinary farmer. Whoever does not establish relative truth and absolute truth as separate, whoever does not abandon samsara to accept nirvana, and whoever does not see that the seed and its result are different is disrespectful to the teaching of general religious philosophy. Whoever does not establish that relative truth and absolute truth are inseparable, whoever does not practice that samsara and nirvana are inseparable, and whoever does not determine that result comes from seed and seed comes from result so that there is no separation between them, is disrespectful to the Great Perfection teaching.

Dharma's respect, which depends on our limitless Wisdom Mind, is disrespectful to samsara's respect, which depends on dualistic mind. If we always respect samsara's way, we cannot release our rigid limited mind into true respectful pure light qualities. But temporarily, as long as we have the phenomenon of relative truth, without respecting samsara's customs, we cannot reveal Dharma's way.

That is why Buddha Shakyamuni said: "Whatever benefits sentient beings benefits the Victorious Ones. Likewise, whatever harms sentient beings harms the Victorious Ones. So therefore, suffering and happiness are equally shared between sentient beings and myself." This does not mean that the Buddha has a dualistic mind like the beings of samsara, sharing unhappiness and happiness, but according to relative truth, the Buddha cannot guide sentient beings to nirvana's qualities without manifesting to the beings of samsara.

If we want to truly show respect, the best practice is to accept a doctrine complementary to our faculties until we have transformed conceptualization into wisdom manifestation, heavy gross elements' disrespect to light subtle elements' respect beyond both disrespect and respect into our pure secret essence.

A paranoid dog's loud barking is disrespectful to thieves but respectful to its master.

Obediently uxorious world leaders are disrespectful to the demands of society's general phenomena but respectful to their self-seeking controlling wives.

Ambitious, unrealized spiritual teachers are disrespectful to the pure Buddhist point of view but respectful to their rich sponsors.

Respect

Bodhisattva's returning flowers after receiving arrows is
    disrespectful to impure worldly custom but respectful to
    pure Bodhisattvas' custom.

Buddha's stainless equanimity wisdom gesture is disrespectful
    to all neurotic dualistic minds separating absolute and
    relative truth but respectful to nondualistic Wisdom Mind,
    in which absolute and relative truth are inseparable.

Tradition

There is no communication in relative truth without
understanding everyone's system and idea, so may I adapt
to everyone's system, wishing for everyone's benefit.

There is no liberation in absolute truth without release
from everyone's system and idea, so may I adapt to
no one's system, beyond benefit's wish.

IN THE WHOLE UNIVERSE no one can agree on one tradition,
but all beings, from small insects to sublime practitioners, depend on some tradition to reach their aim. Without different traditions to choose from, there can be no basis for understanding or
association among beings; there can only be obstacles, chaos, and
misery. Although different groups follow different traditions, all
traditions depend on the energy of the five elements and appear
through different combinations of gross and subtle complementary
elements. But because every tradition has its own individual energy which corresponds to beings' individual faculties it is difficult
for beings to cross from one tradition to another.

For example, spiders have an independent tradition, so they live
alone. They have developed a particular energy and tradition
through their elements that protects them at the same time as it
provides them with food. The spider does not have any servant
tradition, but she can support herself without retinue through her
skillful means energy by surrounding an insect of another tradition
that enters her web. If a spider keeps her own tradition, she is

always comfortable even if she moves; although the place is different the web is the same. But if she tries to change tradition and live in an anthill, it will not work, because ants are holders of a different group tradition which is harmful to spiders.

Because they have a group tradition, ants live in colonies. They have complementary energy through karmic linking, so that with the cooperation of the group they can even take food that is larger than their own body. If they keep their own tradition, it is comfortable for their life, but if they leave their tradition and go to another's, it is harmful for their life. Even if one hundred colonies of ants go to one spider, they will all get stuck in her web. We are talking about general ant's tradition, not giant African ant's tradition.

Even among worldly traditions, there is no agreement on the same subject. It is nice to eat soundlessly sitting at a round table with forks and knives in the polite Western tradition of some countries, and it is nice to eat making delicious sounds, sitting on a cushion with chopsticks in the polite Eastern tradition of some countries. But if we are attached to tradition, when we switch from forks to chopsticks, it is uncomfortable to hold them and hard to make delicious noises with our mouth, and when we switch from chopsticks to forks, it is hard to hold them and be silent.

One country's positive tradition is another country's negative tradition. For example, in the traditions of some countries, if you burp when you eat it means satisfaction and your host says, "Wonderful!" In other countries, if you burp during a meal your host is insulted and you say, "Excuse me!" So there are two different expressions according to traditional habit for one burp.

According to some countries' social customs which are created from childhood by their free speech habit, people are considered inscrutable if they do not talk directly. According to other countries' social customs, people are considered immodest if they do talk directly. So there are two different judgments according to traditional habit for one way of talking.

If we like tradition, the only method is to burp in front of those who like burping and not to burp in front of those who do not like it, just burping temporarily until satisfied, not accepting or rejecting any burping habit, because there is ultimately no benefit from either burping or not burping during the meal. The same is true with talking. The only method is to talk directly in front of those who like it, and to be silent in front of those who do not like it, neither accepting nor rejecting talking or not talking habit.

Even in Dharma, until the dualism of gross and subtle element energy is resolved into one secret essence, different people will follow different traditions. For example, it is the Chinese Taoist T'ai Chi Ch'uan practitioners' tradition to open their anus in order to relax and increase the natural flow of their pure energy. It is the Inner Tantric Yoga practitioners' tradition to close their anus in order to keep vessel air within to increase pure energy.

In the Hinayana tradition, they say that those who are attached to women can never be liberated. According to the Hinayana path, women are supposed to be the source of passions and an obstacle to the moral path. For this reason many Hinayana practitioners become monks and avoid women. In the Inner Tantric tradition, they say that those who do not depend on women can never be liberated. According to the Tantric path, women are the source of wisdom phenomena, and the support of desireless bliss through desire, so many saints revealed that they should be sought as consorts.

Different traditions are suitable to different faculties, so the only method is to accept what we wish, according to our faculties, either Hinayana tradition or Tantric tradition or both. If we fear women, then we can accept the discipline of the Hinayana; if we have love for women, then we can accept the outer complement of the inner wisdom consort of the Tantric tradition; or we can accept both traditions if we can transform the different aspects into one essence.

Ultimately, for the purpose of enlightenment, we must acknowledge traditionless wisdom clear space, which is the source of all countless traditions. But temporarily, while our faculties are obscured, we cannot reject tradition. It is Dharma tradition to say that in order to lead to enlightenment, the Buddha's teaching adapts to worldly customs. Keen pure element faculties always reflect pure Dharma, but those with obstructed impure element faculties cannot adapt to pure Dharma, so they must rely on the traditions of faith until they develop keen faculties.

There are three different kinds of faith: fanatic faith, clear faith, and reasonable faith. If we have fanatic faith, when we see a rock in the road and are told that it is a deity, we pray to it. This fanatic faith may work because our rock phenomena transform into deity phenomena. If we have clear faith, when we go into a temple with a fresh and innocent mind, we accept beautiful frescoes or whatever we see there as positive phenomena. This clear faith works because it creates clear mind. If we have reasonable faith we understand things through logic and can see invisible qualities in visible qualities. For example, if we are in the middle of the ocean and see a duck flying above us in the sky, we have faith that there is land nearby; or if we see smoke behind the mountains, we have faith that there is a fire.

Faith means wishing. If we do not have faith in food's qualities to nourish, why do we wish to eat? If we do not have faith in clothing's qualities to protect our naked bodies, why do we wish to wear clothes? If we do not have faith, how can we make contact with our lovers, our family, our friends, our worldly or Dharma teachers, or our country's custom? If we do not have faith, we are less than animals. Even cows have faith in grass.

If we ask religious people whether they have faith in a god, they say yes. If we ask them if they have faith in their friend, they say no. But the essence of faith is love, so if we really love our god and we really love our friend, then automatically we have faith in both of them. We are just using faith differently according to different traditions. If we think it is nonsense to have faith in a god because a god is invisible, we do not understand that the essence of faith, which is love, is always the same. When we love, we think that we love an object, but really love is inherent within our subject and only reflects to the object. So when love is there, faith is also always there. The object of faith changes from a god, to a country, to a friend, or to a lover according to the tradition we follow, while the temporary and ultimate benefit of faith depends on our intention towards the object.

Tradition

Without depending on tradition we cannot do anything. So until we become enlightened, we cannot reject faith, which depends on tradition. In order to communicate, it is always necessary to deal with society's tradition. But if we rely on it with rigid attachment, then through our clinging, we are trapped by tradition.

The city's street driving tradition is not appropriate if we are driving on a freeway; it puts limits on freedom which are unnecessary. Nevertheless, some rigid Sangha citizens may think that their city street driving habit is always proper anywhere, and want to use it to limit the freedom of people who would rather drive on the open, uncontrived freeways of their Wisdom Minds.

We can say that the purpose of tradition is to invent new forms and new qualities which are more visibly refined in order to reveal the pure light essence of the elements. But because of our habits, we like to hold to only one certain tradition. As tradition holders, we are often afraid of losing our worldly power, so we do not like to change to new qualities. Like most rulers who say that they want to make changes in their government for their public's benefit, we never make them if it means losing our own power. If we change, our phenomena change, and if our phenomena change, there is always a change in the balance of power.

The Dharma point of view is to try to destroy samsara's tradition through wisdom expressions of skillful means such as writing, painting, speaking, or teaching to reach enlightenment, which is beyond tradition. Even so, many generations of artists, philosophers, and teachers have always expressed themselves in the same traditional style. If we write or paint or say something that is not too close to tradition, some rigid Buddhists think it is not the Buddhist point of view. They do not understand that the Buddhist tradition is to break samsara's impure traditions to attain the vastest, purest traditions. Tradition always makes limits if it is not pure. So from the beginning, we should have no attachment to tradition in order to release our mind from the habit of samsara's traditional trap. We should have an understanding of the display of many possible aspects of tradition without ignoring others' traditions in order to benefit and satisfy samsara's traditional beings. In this way, at the same time as we release our mind from tradition, we should play without accepting or rejecting in order to decorate it, as a beautiful bird and a tree each ornament the other.

If as artists we have the limited intention to express only the aesthetic forms within the limits of our tradition, which we see through the obscured eyes of our gross elements, then it is all right for us to be always bound by the limited field of our own country's tradition. If we have the vast intention to be sublime artists, to express the qualities of limitless wisdom tradition, then we must come out of our shadow corner tradition to the center, without rejecting the corner which belongs to the center; and remaining in the light space of the center, we should emanate as many forms as exist unobstructedly.

If as philosophers we have the limited intention to lecture only on gross logical form within the limits of deduction, which we analyze with the neurotic mind of our gross elements, then it is all right for us to be constantly solidifying the reality limits of ordinary beings' invisible phenomena. If we have the vast intention to be sublime philosophers, to create invisible sublime qualities through visible ordinary beings' logic, then we must avoid expectations of externally pompous internally essenceless degrees and titles, and we must pass on the wisdom treasure of our limitless knowledge like a noble river through all the universe's universities, sharing the nectar of our knowledge with all the world's student stream containers.

If as monks we have the limited intention of expressing moral forms within the limits of our tradition which we consider with the moral ego mind of our gross elements, then it is all right for us to be always bound by the useless discipline of our group's tradition. If we have the vast intention to be sublime monks, to accept the limitless tradition of wisdom purity, then we must release ourselves from the cultivated garden of traditional monk's ordinary group organization and go to the stainless vast moral island, letting our morality blossom like a lotus, whose outer and inner petals are both pure and whose unconditioned natural honey perfume emanates unobstructedly to as many fortunate follower bees as exist.

Tradition

If as yogis we have the limited intention to express superstitious forms within the limits of our tradition, which we visualize through the grasping mind of our gross elements, then it is all right for us to be always bound by the limits of positive paranoia. If we have the vast intention to be sublime yogis, to create the limitless uncreated wisdom mandala, then we must escape from complaining ordinary women to join with the desireless great bliss qualities of the full-bodied wish-fulfilling Dakini. Then, drunk with wisdom wine, we can sing realization's songs and awaken wandering beings from heavy elements' ignorance to the light of their natural mind with the sound of the drum and bell.

If as meditators we have the limited intention to only express silent forms within the limits of our breathing, which we inhale and exhale through our limited karmic body's obscured nostrils, then it is all right for us to be always bound by the limited space of our traditional cushions and to be reborn as nearly silent cows, except for an occasional moo. If we have the vast intention to be sublime meditators, then we must release our mind from concentration and relax in infinite natural clear awareness spaceless space. Whatever conceptions of existence and nonexistence arise, we can release them until our thoughts, like self-liberated cloudknots, become light ornaments of traditionless display.

Art

In the crystal mirror theater of Awareness Mind the supreme artist performs his magical displays, but rare is the clear insight audience capable of viewing this wisdom.

A LL ART is composed of subtle and gross elements. There is no way for artists to express without elements. When people use expressions such as hot-headed, cold-hearted, dry-humored, or all wet, it shows that they naturally connect subtle element temperaments with gross element expressions. But artists must go beyond outwardly expressing the elements in an obvious way in order to gain experience with the inner subtle elements, which are the source of the outer gross elements. Then they can make art which reflects what people need.

According to the worldly point of view, artists do not have the ultimate target of reaching enlightenment. They have the temporary purpose of recognizing the inner emotions and then expressing these externally. Ordinary artists usually express themselves for communication, fame, or power. Because they feel isolated, they want to connect with the external world through art for their own benefit. Because they are not connected to a source beyond their own intellect or tradition, they cannot deeply explain to others what their work is about. They just make art which becomes the master controlling them. If they do not express themselves with a wisdom point of view, the result is always impermanence and diminishing energy which leads to suffering.

According to the Buddhist point of view, an artist's intention is compassion. Buddhist artists create in order to make a link with other beings through their inner pure elements, and to transform their outer ordinary gross elements into enlightenment by means of that connection. In the Tantric system, artists express the quality of the pure energy of the inner elements externally through images and statues representing form; through teachings, songs, poems, and music representing speech; through dances representing activities; and through infinite harmonious manifestations representing mind. Because they are connected to its source they can always deeply explain to others what their work is about and are always the master in control of their art. Through the sublime artists' intentions, the outer gross elements are purified into the inner subtle elements and reconnect with inner wisdom phenomena. Temporarily, this gives satisfaction because one recognizes the inner qualities in the outer expression of art. Ultimately, there is liberation through the purification of essenceless art's substance into substanceless essence enlightenment.

Wisdom Mind cannot be seen unless we have wisdom eyes. The basic natural pure element colors cannot be seen but are dormant, pervading everywhere and always moving. Through this movement different elements connect, becoming visible form and color. The root colors are blue, white, red, yellow, and green. Just as each element contains all the other elements, each color contains all the other colors. So each of the root colors has five branch colors which depend on the elements' changing contributing circumstances and connections. As they connect and change, countless new branches of color are created until they become so subtle that their relation to the original root color can hardly be recognized. Ordinary eyes cannot see pure natural light. Because of their obscured vision, they can only see colors as stale, pale, and diminished compared to these inherently pure root colors. But with wisdom eyes, the original natural source colors are recognized, and through this connection to pure color root circumstances, pure phenomena naturally increase with contributing circumstances.

The imagination of ordinary artists can become exhausted when their vision becomes more and more obscured from the pure natural source of color. Since they do not believe in the inner invisible pure essence of form and color, they must go back to gross external phenomena which they can see with their gross element eyes for the source of their visual ideas. But because they only depend on inflexible gross element form and color, their minds become rigid and limited. Their conceptions are confused, so they cannot create vast space in their art and it becomes inflexible, crowded, and stuck. Because sublime artists recognize the pure invisible essence of the elements, they understand that the natural source color is always undiminished and they can make fresh dynamic form and color from the invisible again and again in their art. Because they have vast unobstructed minds, they understand how to create vast space in their art and they can create any phenomena.

In this way, if artists recognize the source of conceptions, when they express them, the connection between the conception and its source will be unbroken and therefore pure, fresh, and light. Because the lineage of artists depends on conception and conception depends on the elements, by understanding the source of conception, artists can understand the essence of color. For example, if artists understand the conception of anger, they know that its source is the fire element and can be expressed through the color red. If they understand desire or nervousness, they know that its source is the water or air element and can be expressed through movement. If this movement is depressed or frustrated, then its appropriate color is blue or green; if it is elated, its color is luminous and clear. If they understand indifferent or foggy mind, they know that its source is the earth element and can express calm, dull, or heavy qualities in a person through a pale yellow color. The color of each element depends on the balance of the other elements which exist within it inconspicuously. For example, soil whose elements are complementary and which does not depend on fertilizer for its freshness is often a deep red color.

If artists do not perceive the pure sounds, colors, and motions of the light subtle elements inherent in the external gross elements, they cannot capture the essence of whatever they want to depict or convey. By only believing in the visible and denying the invisible, they cannot express the vitality of life, whose source is within invisible light, and their art will be static and lifeless.

The sublime artist, like the sublime visualizer, views phenomena from the sublime point of view of actual relative truth, which does not separate subtle from gross or invisible from visible. The artist is like the visualizer, but the artist uses substance means to make the invisible conspicuous, while the visualizer uses subtle means to make the invisible conspicuous. The purpose of both is to reach the invisible through the visible.

If artists want to depict something, they must first examine the gross visible elements of form in order to show their subject's invisible subtle elements. With the confidence that comes from subtle elements' experience sublime artists can understand the gross elements and play spontaneously. They do not need to judge between truth and fantasy because, from the sublime point of view of actual relative truth, subtle substanceless fantasy and gross substance reality existing within deluded mind are equally untrue. Because of this, artists do not need to worry whether they are expressing what is true or what is untrue. If they just depict everything as art, it will definitely suit somewhere.

In the Buddhist tradition, art can be made to express the ugly or the beautiful, the calm or the turbulent. Sublime artists who recognize the needs of other beings can combine turbulent or calm elements to achieve a result appropriate to the circumstances. If an antidote for depression whose cause is elation is needed, the sublime artist can make sad or ugly things to remind one of the weariness of samsara through images expressing the sad or ugly aspects of existence. They are intended as a compassionate warning, like a parent's protective anger, helping us to recognize and to be repelled by the form of rebirth that results from bad intentions such as anger and hatred. If an antidote for elation whose cause is depression is needed, the sublime artist can make pleasant or beautiful things. Beautiful images are made to help with good habits, to remove people from negative intentions through the recognition of perfection.

According to the Tantric system, there are countless manifestations, which can all be contained within two aspects: peaceful and wrathful. These originate from Dharmakaya or clear space.

According to Wisdom Mind, the peaceful aspect arises from the inherently unobscured nature of the luminous essence of the pure earth and water elements, which are inseparable from the beginning. This pure wisdom essence has the quality of unobscured boundless expanse.

From the point of view of ordinary mind, the earth and water elements both have the visible and touchable qualities of form in its gross aspect. Even so, they are still permeated by the unobscured boundless qualities of space. The nature of ordinary form is impermanence. When the gross elements diminish and their form decays, suffering always results. By transforming the outer gross elements into their own pure luminous essence, which is indestructible, suffering is removed. This can be learned by practicing to internalize the familiar form of the external gross images perceived through the senses and retaining only their light essence in the mind. Through this practice, gross form is transformed and purified into light becoming increasingly like deity phenomena.

Form is expressed by the Tantric artist in the beautiful qualities of desirable objects. These are expressed by the artist in the form of attractive peaceful deities representing whatever sentient beings desire to touch through grasping. In samsara, this results in the ordinary bliss of desire, which is always the cause of suffering because of its impermanent, changeable nature. But as the object of desire is purified and transformed through visualization and meditation from substance into the light and untouchable essence of the subtle elements, desire becomes desireless. In this way, through compassion, the artist has shown the path to desireless bliss, which is beyond destruction and the suffering of samsara.

According to Wisdom Mind, the wrathful deity aspect arises from the inherently unobstructed nature of the luminous essence of the pure fire and air elements, which are inseparable from the beginning. This pure wisdom essence has the quality of unobstructed clear effortless expression, which is characteristic of pure sound, whose essence is harmonious and light.

From the point of view of ordinary mind, the fire and air elements both have qualities which are symbolic of sound in its gross aspect. Even so, they are still permeated by the unobstructed and untouchable qualities of pure sound. The nature of ordinary sound is impermanence, and being impermanent, it has the tendency to diminish, which leads to suffering.

In general, the antidote to wrath is peace, as fire's antidote is water. But sometimes violent beings cannot be purified by peaceful forms and need wrathful forms, just as iron can only be broken by a harder metal such as steel. The Tantric artist can provide an antidote to the violent energy of these beings by expressing the pure energy of unobstructed wisdom qualities in the forms of wrathful images, sounds, and activities. Even if ordinary anger based on aversion arises, since wrath is related to the fire element, whose essence is clarity, this clarity can burn the impure turbulent phenomena of the jungle of conceptions into pure wisdom fire and air elements, which are inseparable, revealing wisdom clarity.

According to the Great Vehicle teaching, sublime art removes obstacles by breaking inert, obsolete, samsaric traditions to make unobstructed deities' traditionless space through pure tradition. In this way it creates countless qualities which clearly reflect the Buddha's vast wisdom space.

Sublime artists always give energy to others through their art. When they die, they do not leave ordinary inert substance art as a lifeless remainder, but their pure spiritual power lives in their art for the benefit of others. Even a detail like water or a tree created by a sublime artist can help and bless those who perceive it. That is what the Buddha Shakyamuni meant when he said: "I emanate a countless variety of forms for the benefit of all sentient beings." Ultimately, we cannot judge who is the greatest artist. Whoever gives energy to others through their art is a great artist.

Basically, the structure of the artist's system is the same whether ordinary or sublime. Art comes from the inner elements and is expressed externally for the purpose of being absorbed again in the inner mind in order to increase externally again and so on in an unending circle. The difference between the ordinary and sublime artist lies in the point of view.

For those with an ordinary point of view, the unending circle is

the circle of suffering in samsara. For those artists who understand
the sublime wisdom point of view, the pure light spiritual energy
moves in an unending wisdom circle, a mandala of the deity. It is
inexhaustible, never trapped and never obscured. Since the energy
is pure, whatever aspect manifests is always clear. It is unending
because the birth and death of beings never ends until all are enlightened.

> Endless horrible things of samsara
> Endless wonderful things of nirvana
> Drawn by the mind.
>
> So the mind is the greatest artist
> Painting various relative truths
> With the brush of conception.
>
> If we are not deluded
> By the various colors of the different natural elements
> As they appear on the unobstructed mirror of the mind,
> Then nature is always clear space
> And there is no confusion.
>
> Various phenomena, a youthful prince
> Married to untouchable emptiness,
> A smooth and mysterious princess,
> From their joyful inseparable union
> Many generations of phenomena are increased
> In a continuing display
> For the comfort of their pitiful subjects.

Isolation

One who can remain alone in stainless mind
is the continuous Buddha.
If I need a friend, then I must find one
who can adapt to me, who can comfort me, and
who can be a support to my enlightenment.
But just one other person can
cause attachment and hatred,
and between attachment and hatred
there is always suffering.
So I had better try to isolate myself
like a wounded deer.
O Lord Buddha,
please remain in my heart always.

ALL BEINGS have in their minds the seed of isolation. Though we may not want to be isolated, from the beginning we are born alone and in the end we must die alone and be separated from others. We become isolated if the elements of those around us do not complement our own. Our minds contain both pure and impure elements, which are constantly increasing or diminishing. We become isolated when the pure light subtle elements are more abundant that the impure heavy gross elements, and the impure heavy gross elements cannot complement their energy or find support in other similar gross elements. We become isolated when the impure heavy gross elements are more abundant than the pure light subtle elements, and the pure light subtle elements cannot complement their energy or find a support in other similar subtle elements.

There can be isolation without intention or with intention. Some ordinary beings who do not intend to be violent in this life are isolated without intention because through the karmic result of their previous lives' violent intention, they are born with harmful uncomplementary gross elements and violent energy, which causes everyone to abandon them. Certain wild animals are like this. Other animals either run from them or group together to annihilate them. There is no benefit to this kind of isolation, so it is meaningless and very sad. Temporarily it brings only suffering because the energy of these beings cannot complement the elements of others, and ultimately it brings only suffering because there is no support for them to change and connect with positive phenomena.

Usually violent beings can only change by depending on the help of very kind and gentle beings. Sometimes, though, if they are not powerful enough, the light elements of gentle beings can be harmed by the heavy elements of violent beings, the way a fresh young plant is injured by pouring boiling water on it. But if through previous experience, gentle beings' pure light element energy is more powerful than heavy element violent energy, they can support and benefit violent beings by softening their heavier elements as leather can be softened with butter. If we continuously put fire under water, it boils, becoming more and more turbulent and dry, finally exhausting itself. But if we add cold water, the turbulence subsides and the water does not diminish. So, eventually, whatever the method, violent beings must accept the energy and help of gentle beings.

Some ordinary beings are isolated without intention because their elements no longer link with the elements of others. They may be hurt like a wounded animal and need isolation in order to protect themselves, or they may be old and unable to connect with the elements of others because their energy has become diminished and, being tired, they need isolation in order to rest.

Some beings who are isolated without intention are sublime, like the Buddha. Because their energy is totally light and pure, the heavy obstructed elements of ordinary beings cannot complement their vast qualities. They are isolated according to ordinary general phenomena, but according to their personal wisdom phenomena, there is no conception of isolation or nonisolation. For this reason the Buddha Shakyamuni was isolated from his kingdom because the ordinary energy of his subjects could not complement his extraordinary sublime energy.

Beings who have wisdom intelligence often become isolated eccentrics because ordinary-minded people cannot accept their Wisdom Mind phenomena. Only other sublime-minded people can accept their eccentric phenomena, which to them is not eccentric. For instance, people with eccentric wisdom intelligence may be bored with endless explanations of ordinary-minded farmers who say, "I plowed my field, I planted my seed, I watched my plants grow, and when they ripened, I ate them." They can synthesize this whole process into one essence and say, "I eat earth." People with ordinary minds think this sounds stupid because their ordinary intelligence cannot instantly understand the essence of things.

If wisdom eccentrics say that grass is butter, ordinary narrow-minded people think they are crazy. But because wisdom eccentrics see that all gross substance exists through the linking of inner and outer elements, they know that when cows eat grass they give milk, which is later turned into butter. Because wisdom eccentrics see all the connections between the visible and invisible elements, they want to express what is true according to sublime actual relative truth. People with ordinary intelligence also want to say what is true, but they do not understand these connections, so according to wisdom eccentrics, they only accept inverted relative truth, thinking it is ordinary actual relative truth.

Some people with ordinary intelligence are also eccentric. Often we do not like to show our eccentricity because we do not like to be isolated. This does not mean that we want to be with people because we have compassion for them. It means that because we are afraid, we are always depending on others, because we do not have the confidence to be independent, are afraid of separation. Even if the minority's view is correct, we still hold on to the majority's view through fear of isolation.

There was once a king who asked his astrologer to calculate his country's future. The astrologer predicted that in one week rain would fall which would poison all the water in the kingdom, making everyone who drank it crazy. This powerful king was just an ordinary selfish king, and so he thought first and only of himself. To protect himself, he covered his well from the rain but did not warn his subjects to protect their water. Soon, as the astrologer predicted, the rain came and poisoned the water and all the subjects became crazy. Since the king's personal phenomena seemed different from the subjects' general phenomena, the subjects grew paranoid toward him. Even though the expressions of the king's personal phenomena were true according to ordinary actual relative truth, because his subjects' minds were deluded, they thought that he was crazy and that all his ideas, actions, and words were untrue. Then all these crazy subjects tried to abandon him, and the king became isolated and had no power. But he was so afraid of being isolated that he drank the poisoned water and connected with their crazy deluded minds in ordinary inverted relative truth phenomena.

Eccentric people who have confidence in their Wisdom Mind are not afraid of isolation and often isolate themselves intentionally. Many people think that to practice Dharma we must be isolated. But although may saints temporarily isolated themselves to practice Dharma, they did not do so in order to be ultimately isolated. They only isolated themselves outwardly in order to increase the vast pure inner elements of their wish-fulfilling Wisdom Mind, which has endless qualities that are never isolated.

> Isolated and fragile like the earthworm, when we are born from the womb, we cannot move freely, we cannot breathe freely.
> Isolated and ruined like a caved-in-house, when we take our death sigh, we cannot move freely, we cannot breathe freely.
> Between isolated birth and isolated death, we try to join

with others, but always we are in great isolation meaninglessly.

When we are infants we are isolated because we cannot speak with others.

When we start to speak, our parents teach us to say hello, which automatically means they are teaching us to say good-bye.

When we are taught to say good-bye, this automatically means departure to an essenceless destination, which means isolation.

When we meet someone, we say "How are you," which automatically means that one day we will be pale-cheeked patients with tears dropping from pitiful faces, isolated in bed.

It is so sad because still we do not recognize that everything naturally goes toward isolation.

When we love we say "I love you," which automatically means we are afraid, we don't love.

We are isolated when we say "I love you." We say "I love you" to escape from our isolation.

When we are old people with puffy eyes and haggard mouths, we are isolated from neglecting young people.

From beginningless time until now, all ignorant sentient beings tried to find company, but we are always isolated meaninglessly because we disobeyed our Self-Awareness Noble Mother's advice.

Even though we are isolated, there is no meaning to our isolation, just like a wounded deer is isolated from his herd temporarily for protection from violent hunters and ultimately because he lacks confidence about where to go.

From isolated feeling, we create more and more isolation.

If we are afraid to be isolated, if we do not want to be isolated, we must go into isolation like sublime beings in ancients times.

Buddha Shakyamuni left his elaborate kingdom and young companions to go into isolation under the Bodhi tree with rugged clothes. But his samadhi isolation is meaningful because, to comfort sentient beings from his wisdom samadhi, he found omniscient Buddha company always smiling from the ten directions.

Padmasambhava was banished by Oddiyana's palace and stayed in isolation in many graveyards. But his realization isolation is meaningful because, to help sentient beings through his wisdom phenomena, he found Wisdom Dakini company dancing in all universes.

Milarepa was betrayed by his uncle and aunt and through aversion for samsara went into isolation in a cave for his whole life. But his Mahamudra isolation is meaningful because, to benefit sentient beings through his realization hymns, he found the face of Dharmakaya everywhere.

Longchenpa left samsara's impure rejection phenomena to go into isolation with his one rugged sack in the snowcapped mountains to see nirvana's pure acceptance phenomena. But his Mahasandhi isolation is meaningful because, to give inexhaustibly to sentient beings his priceless jewel teaching from his Wisdom Clear Sky Mind, he found all equanimity display of countless stars beyond pure and impure acceptance-rejection phenomena.

Meditation Practice

My grandfather of mindfulness must watch constantly after this spoiled child of deluded mind to save him from disaster.

★ ★ ★

Many saints have said, if you really want to practice, you must always remain in one place until you reach enlightenment. But even though I remain in one place just as they said, my distracted fantasy mind flies in the ten directions. I think maybe the saints are judging from their own experience according to their own faculties, because for me nothing works if I cannot lure my eagle ego into the samadhi cage through concentration. So I had better fly in the ten directions even though I have lost the social custom and people call me aimless.

Many saints have said, if you really want to practice, you must always wander in uncertain places. But even though I wander as they said, my distracted fantasy mind exhausts itself in the ten directions. I think maybe the saints are judging from their own experience according to their own faculties, because for me nothing works if I cannot tame my wild horse ego into the samadhi stable. So I had better stay in one place even though I have lost the gypsy custom and people call me lazy.

INSTEAD of really practicing Dharma, we often only talk about practicing Dharma. The more we talk without practicing, the more we lose our energy in words, and so the more our point of view is lost. According to the Buddhist path, if we are true practitioners, whether we are praying, offering, or practicing yoga, visualization, or meditation, the essence is always the unobscured, established point of view. It is best to remember that, for practitioners, the point of view is beyond description.

There was once a flock of cranes who were flying south. Their leader told them, "Don't make any sound or we will be killed by human beings." So all the cranes started saying, "Don't make any sound! Don't make any sound! Don't make any sound!" until there was no silence in the sky. Even though there is no need to use words to describe our realization, still words automatically come more and more to describe our descriptionless mind.

Inner yoga breathing exercises use the five elements inherent within air, purifying the gross elements into the naturally subtle elements and then into the secret essence of the elements. Earth air, water air, fire air, wind air, and space air can be used by inner yoga practitioners who do not want to depend on medicines as antidotes to their illnesses. A yogi can purify his impure stale earth air elements by visualizing and inhaling pure fresh yellow earth air. He can purify his impure heavy water air elements by visualizing and inhaling pure white water air. He can purify his impure smoky fire air elements by visualizing and inhaling pure red fire air. He can purify his impure unclear wind air elements by visualizing and inhaling pure green wind air. He can purify his impure dullness space air elements by visualizing light untouchable form and inhaling pure clear blue space air.

Yoga exercises can be helpful to a person with an uncomfortable, badly proportioned body. Since the heavy and visible gross elements are the source of these qualities, the person who believes in and depends on the light and invisible subtle elements may temporarily gain a comfortable, well-proportioned body for this present life. When the yoga practitioner purifies the gross elements, the light elements in his body become visible. But if he only has faith in the gross and subtle elements of his own body and not in the secret vast essence which pervades everywhere, his point of view is limited, and since the benefit of his exercise is limited to his own body, he can never attain Wisdom Deity body.

Even without believing in the secret wisdom potential of the elements, by making their bodies lighter, some gymnasts who have practiced yoga show that they can find the subtle elements within the gross elements. Through their activities they automatically reveal their stamina and the vital capacities existing dormantly within, which arise from the original nature of their elements. Perfecting their bodies through the light elements, they play and compete with other light element bodies in front of gross element spectators, who watch with gross element eyes and award gross element medals, really meaning "Thank you so much for letting me see your light elements."

Buddhist practitioners who believe in deity phenomena understand that they are light, invisible, unobstructed, and can miraculously appear anywhere because they pervade everywhere. Because of this, they acknowledge the secret wisdom potential of the elements within their own bodies and practice with visualization, sadhana, and mudra. They visualize pure essence deity phenomena to subdue their impure gross elements and to allow the secret essence of their elements to manifest. As a result, their present life's body becomes well proportioned and comfortable, and their after-life's body becomes Wisdom Deity body. These practitioners do not get a gross element medal from a gross element audience. Their only reward is wisdom praise and they are showered with flowers of light from Buddhas, Bodhisattvas, saints, and all wise persons because their Wisdom Deity phenomena go everywhere unobstructedly for the benefit of everyone.

If we wish to attain Wisdom Deity speech, we must purify our gross and subtle elements. Those who do breathing, yoga, or dance exercises are especially adept at purifying their gross elements into light elements, so their sound becomes resonant and clear as their earth elements' nerves become transparent like crystal. Consequently, their water elements become very pure, their air elements become very light, and their ordinary conceptions are transformed into unobscured wisdom clarity. In this way, words are always true and meaningful and very light. Those who speak like this are naturally and unintentionally attractive, and whoever hears their speech is drawn to them.

Buddha's speech has countless qualities which can be contained within two qualities: inconceivably secret speech and the expression of all existing aspects. Inconceivably secret speech is so deep that it has no front, no back, no center, no beginning, and no end according to absolute truth. Because it has no limit or time or direction or any kind of obscuration, it is beyond any examination by logic and deduction. The expression of all existing aspects includes any Dharma or non-Dharma words, which always benefit by reflecting an aspect of truth according to pure actual relative truth.

These two qualities are inseparable according to the Buddha's teaching. They do not have divided dualistic sound as our ordinary words do. Because we have become separated from the pure essence of the elements which is within nondualistic mind, we continue to divide the elements, making them grosser and grosser. Then, when our inner and outer elements are subdivided so many times that the divisions cannot catch and connect with each other, our speech becomes untruthful. As a result, when outer object elements arise, inner subject elements are missing; when inner subject elements arise, outer object elements are missing, and when both arise, one diminishes and becomes less powerful than the other. In this way, whatever is said automatically becomes untruthful. That is why at one moment we say: "Please tell me whatever I can do for you," and the next moment we say, "I'm sorry, I cannot do anything for you."

Within Tantric practice, visualizers can use different names depending on their path, such as deity's body, deity's speech, deity's mind, and pure land's source of the seed of body, speech, and mind. There is a syllable called Palace of the Deity's Letter which contains countless letters coming from unobstructed, mirrorlike awareness mind. Whether created or not created, deluded or undeluded, because this syllable is unobstructed, countless letters still come from it, so it is called Emanation of Letters. Whether circumstances are gathered or not, if we examine deeply and still cannot find any sound, this is called Great Meaningful Unborn Letter, the source of all endless letters.

We sentient beings never use unborn letters. Our letters always come through circumstances, are always born, and therefore are always diminishing. Because there is no truth between being born and diminished and because as a result of karma, sentient beings do not understand the elements which create speech, Emanation of Letters becomes obscured and seems obstructed. Because pure natural absolute truth is obscured between being born and diminishing, there is no pure actual relative truth. So whether we talk sweetly or harshly, we only make the same meaningless, shallow, deluded, noisy, limited expression, the cause of elation, depression, or stupor.

All speech comes from the energy of the five elements. The pronunciation of vowels and consonants comes from the activities of different elements according to different languages, different realms of existence, and different individuals' karmic elements. They are too numerous to discuss here, but to give a general example: in English, the letter *A* comes predominantly from the air and space elements; the letter *B* comes predominantly from the earth element; the letter *C* comes predominantly from the air element; the letter *D* comes predominantly from the earth and air elements, and the letter *E* comes predominantly from the air and fire elements. In this way, sound is born from different sources.

If the elements of the karmic body are not pure, then words are not clear. For instance, if the nerves which are related to the earth element are not pure, they become knotted, and because of this circumstance, the blood, which is related to the water element, becomes clotted and does not flow smoothly. When the blood is thick and unclear, influenced by external circumstances like fire element turbulence, excitement, or anxiety, it can result in high blood pressure, which causes the air element to become obstructed. As all the elements become turbulent, crowded, and uncomplementary, the tongue becomes rigid and cannot move appropriately. As the blood is pushed up to the throat, if the fire elements are too heated, the voice becomes scratchy, and although it is possible to talk, the sound is not smooth. If the veins, which are related to the earth element, are not smooth, they swell. As a result, the openings to the air and water elements become blocked and people become mute.

If the elements are balanced and light, the blood and air elements flow smoothly and the voice is melodious. Those whose air elements are pure will have an especially good tone when they sing or talk, although the quality of their words will depend on their inner spiritual qualities. If they have pure inner subtle spiritual elements, whatever they say is very meaningful and beautiful, always like poetry and song.

Of course, if we like, according to our personal phenomena and our individual faculties, we can choose any system or tradition of practice we wish or need that is available within general phenomena. Among these, certain traditions and texts have a symbolic point of view which teaches visualization of colors, forms, signs, and symbols. The real purpose of this symbolic point of view is to reveal through skillful means the essence within deity's wisdom display. Then even though we hold a walking stick in our hand, it can become a wisdom sword. Even though we hold nothing in our hand, still there is a wisdom sword which spontaneously cuts the residual net of neurotic contradictory conceptions of deluded dualistic mind.

Within samsara, one tool cannot penetrate everywhere. The many aspects of gross elements require many different tools, so the Buddha manifested many tools, not just one sword or one symbol but swords without limit. We make a limit if we completely trust one graspable knife or one breakable vessel. But wisdom is never limited. We use certain particular sadhanas and texts to realize unobstructed limitless wisdom display. If we do not use our own inherent wisdom weapons, we must rely on symbolic weapons to destroy obstructions. But symbolic weapons are limited. If we realize our inherent wisdom weapon, we can penetrate everywhere without limited gross element means.

In general, Buddhists practice to subdue their minds. They are meditating in order to purify the heavy gross elements into the light subtle elements and then into their pure secret essence, in order not to remain in dull empty space. Through meditation, Buddhists want to know stainless Wisdom Awareness Mind, which has unobstructed, pure, light qualities.

On the path of meditation we can experience bliss in our body. This bliss experience is predominantly a blend of bliss and desire, which has the potential energy of the water element. If we become attached to our experience of bliss, we will be reborn in the desire realm of the gods. This attachment of the obscured mind to bliss has the potential solid energy of the earth element. However, if we do not become attached to our experience of bliss, but continue to use it as a support for attaining indestructible wisdom body, the earth and water elements become lighter and lighter and purer and purer, and our body becomes lighter, reflecting the potential of our increasing inner bliss. Through the natural pure power of wisdom bliss and sublime light form, the conflicting impure desire elements of beings, especially god-realm beings, are purified, and they are automatically drawn into a state of blissful empty luminosity. Gradually, as the distinction between the earth and water elements disappears, we have the experience of bliss without attachment.

On the path of meditation we can experience clarity in our speech. This clarity experience is predominantly a blend of clarity and anger, which has the potential energy of the fire element. If we become attached to this experience of clarity, we will be reborn in the form realm of the gods. This attachment of the obscured mind to clarity has the potential active energy of the air element. However, if we do not become attached to our experience of clarity, but continue to use it as a support for attaining desireless wisdom speech, the fire and air elements become lighter and lighter and purer and purer, and our speech becomes more melodious, reflecting the potential of our increasing inner clarity. Through the natural pure power of wisdom clarity and sublime melodious speech, the conflicting impure anger elements of beings, especially god-realm beings, are purified, and they are automatically drawn into a state of stainless empty luminosity. Gradually, as the distinction between the fire and air elements disappears, we have the experience of clarity without attachment.

On the path of meditation we can experience emptiness in our mind. This emptiness experience is predominantly a blend of emptiness and ignorance which has the potential energy of the space element. If we become attached to this experience of emptiness, we will be reborn in the formless realm of the gods. However, if we do not become attached to this experience of emptiness, but continue to use it as a support for attaining Self-Awareness Wisdom Mind, the space element becomes lighter and lighter and purer and purer, and our mind temporarily becomes sublime, reflecting the potential of our increasing inner emptiness. Through the natural pure power of wisdom space and sublime unborn mind, the conflicting impure ignorance elements of beings, especially god-realm beings, are purified, and they are automatically drawn into a state of undeluded awareness emptiness. Gradually, as the distinction between outer and inner space elements disappears, we have the experience of emptiness without attachment.

Within the energy of the elements, there are gross and subtle conceptions. Gross conceptions relate to the heavy gross elements, and subtle conceptions relate to the light subtle elements. In general, when we meditate, we watch our mind and can directly recognize gross conceptions through feelings or passions as they arise. By recognizing these gross conceptions, we can be liberated from them. In meditation when we think we are having fewer conceptions, it is usually the gross conceptions which are diminishing, while the undercurrent of subtle ones continues to move unrecognized, like the subtle activity of springs under the still surface of a pond covered with husks of grain. Because it is so difficult to recognize, the subtle activity of the mind is always dangerous and is the seed of the passions, which create gross phenomena. To purify these subtle element conceptions, beginning practitioners must depend on remembering mind or mindfulness.

According to the different teachings, all kinds of mindfulness can be contained within mindfulness of perception and mindfulness of dharmata. Mindfulness of perception is the reliance on watching the mind with concentration during meditation. This kind of perception is not like ordinary perception, which concentrates on external objects and clings to them; instead, it concentrates on the subject through the senses or circumstances. Concentration or perception with mindfulness has the temporary benefit of maintaining a calm and stable mind, not easily fooled into action by objects.

We depend on mindfulness of perception until we obtain mindfulness of dharmata. Dharmata is the essential, natural character of phenomena, the source of purity in the elements, the unconditioned self-nature of mind. Mindfulness of dharmata is effortless and does not depend on concentration because it is completely natural. The ultimate benefit of mindfulness is the joining of our mind's impure, conditioned elements to the unconditioned mindfulness of dharmata, which is inseparable from natural secret essence awareness. So, until we have the confidence of the mindfulness of dharmata, we must always rely on the mindfulness of perception.

Mindfulness is most important in practice, of course, but it is also necessary in worldly affairs. Without mindfulness, nothing can be accomplished; we would miss the time, lose the meaning of words, miscalculate everything, and always miss the target.

Once a fighting match was arranged between a powerful giant wrestler and a slight gymnast. The night before the fight, the gymnast was anxious and could not sleep, worrying about the wrestler's size. When his wife asked him why he was so anxious, he told her about his opponent's strength and said, "I will definitely lose tomorrow." His wife comforted him and said, "Do not worry. Tomorrow I will sing a song from the audience. Do not be distracted by my voice. Concentrate on the fight, and when you hear me sing, grab the giant's testicles and squeeze as hard as you can until he falls down."

The next day as they were fighting and the giant was winning, the wife began to sing, "Giant, you are so splendid and powerful, but one of your precious jewels is about to fall from your forehead." The giant immediately grabbed his forehead, leaving himself only one hand to fight with. At that, the agile gymnast concentrated as his wife had instructed and, squeezing with all his might, made the giant fall down.

With his last breath, as he lay dying, the giant answered the wife's song, saying, "The most powerful giant who lost his mindfulness has been killed by a slight opponent who kept his mindfulness. My life has ended today because mindlessly I grasped for the deceiving fantasy jewel which I forgot I had from the beginning, and so I lost the jewel of my mindfulness. There is no jewel more precious than the most precious jewel of mindfulness." Then he died.

According to different texts, for different faculties there are many methods of liberating conceptions through mindfulness. Usually meditators watch conceptions, examining where they come from, where they go to, and where they remain. This is good for the beginning meditator, but it is not good to be always examining. Since mind is unobstructed, conceptions arise continuously. By constantly examining them, we never relax and only create new conceptions. After dissolving conceptions through examining them, they arise again, making the process of examining exhausting. Between the antidote conception of examining and the object of the antidote conception, the mind is never calm, even if the physical posture looks restful.

If the ordinary mind is never calm, we cannot see our true natural mind. Some minds have more subtle activity than others, even though on their surface they appear calm. To calm this subtle activity, it is most important when meditating to try to relax the mind. But when the beginning meditator tries to relax, more conceptions than usual seem to arise. We expect our mind to be more peaceful, so when these many conceptions arise, we become discouraged with meditation.

This kind of beginning meditator becomes discouraged through substance habit greed or ignorance about the karmic system. Greed comes from having always been involved with tangible gross element substance, so that when we meditate, we follow this same habit by wanting to touch and use our conceptions easily. Our calculations are based on machine habits. This is especially true in a materially powerful country which is rich in substance and technology and whose people from infancy have an easy life. For those of us who grow up with this machine habit, it is difficult to make our minds calm immediately. Since we try to understand substanceless light elements through substance conceptions, we cannot release these conceptions, and soon we abandon meditation. The karmic system explains that over countless lives in samsara we have created countless habits and conceptions that obscure our natural secret Wisdom Mind. So in this life, even if we are trying to meditate, the countless dormant conceptions from our countless previous lives arise and disturb our meditation. Then we become very discouraged because in one moment we have not dispelled the conceptions of our countless previous lives.

We must meditate continuously without impatience and stubborn stupidity, with the guidance of a wisdom teacher or a compassionate spiritual friend who has natural wisdom power and experience about sublime spiritual qualities. We must meditate with skillful means, not by hoping to liberate our conceptions immediately or to reach enlightenment immediately. It is also not necessary to hope that one day far in the future, through patience or intelligence in our meditation, we may reach enlightenment. We must not calculate future or immediate time in our meditation. This expectation only makes us hysterical. If we expect enlightenment right now, then enlightenment goes farther and farther away. If we assume that enlightenment is far away, then again we create far-away conceptions and enlightenment goes farther and farther away. These calculations create distance, time, and boundaries.

If we really want to be sublime meditators, we should not set a time period for our meditation as is the modern meditator's style. We should not count the hours or minutes, because limited time makes limited meditation. Our ordering, limited gross and subtle elements' mind cannot release itself into the sublime, limitless, secret essence of the elements if we are bound by exact time. If our mind is bound by anything, it is never vast. If we are always trapped and limited by time, place, and direction, how can we have Wisdom Mind confidence? How can we understand other people's faculties and benefit other beings? How can we help limited mind with limited meditation mind?

An endlessly flowing river never diminishes no matter how

much it is used, because it is always replenished by its deep source. Even though it appears the same as the endless river, a river which flows from an artificial reservoir has no deep source and in time is exhausted. If we depend on the gross and subtle elements without recognizing their secret essence, our energy will be shallow and quickly exhausted like the artificial reservoir. Even though we might think we are helping other people through gross element intelligence, if we do not have wisdom confidence, our help is only shallow and temporary. If we depend on the secret essence of our elements, our energy will flow endlessly like the endless river.

Meditation is necessary to open channels and veins for the circulation of air. The mind depends on this. If the beginning meditator has a balanced posture, then the channels and nerves are straight and open, the circulation of air is unobstructed, and the mind can become balanced. If we want a meaningful posture, we must concentrate not just on our body's posture, but also on our mind's posture. Mind is one mind. When we meditate we must not concentrate on an object or search for a subject. We should not have modern brain habit mind, and we should not have ancient heart habit mind. We should only relax and separate ourselves from the five skandhas and remain in nondualistic mind.

The essential characteristic of meditation is that it is free from the essential characteristics of each of the five skandhas. Destructibility or receptivity is the essential characteristic of the skandha of form, whose conspicuous gross element is earth. Gathering, experiencing, or the movement of desire is the essential characteristic of the skandha of feeling, whose conspicuous gross element is water. Ripening, understanding, or pursuing an object is the essential characteristic of the skandha of perception, whose conspicuous gross element is fire. Increasing actions and accumulating tendencies is the essential characteristic of the skandha of intention, whose conspicuous gross element is air. Perception and creation of objects is the essential characteristic of the skandha of consciousness, whose conspicuous gross element is space.

According to the Mahayana system, especially Madhyamika meditation, practitioners predominantly try to meditate in emptiness, which is free from all mental activity. All mental activity can be contained in the five skandhas. Whenever we are free from the five skandhas, we recognize our Clear Space Sky Mind.

From the beginning, basic limitless great emptiness mind is inherent within the limited path emptiness of the practitioner. If in this life we meditate in great emptiness, gradually both our daytime phenomena and our dream phenomena disappear and become the same, so there is no more between. Then at death when we separate from our karmic body, there is no more next life's conception phenomena, only clear wisdom space. In the same way, the space inside a pot is no different from the space outside a pot. When we break the pot, pot space is not lost because pot space is the same as all space. It is only the substance elements of the pot which give it the appearance of being different. If we have confidence, there is no more path emptiness, but only its result, which is stainless great emptiness, inseparable from basis emptiness.

According to the General Tantric system, practitioners predominantly try to meditate into luminosity. Depending on their deity's sadhana or practice, through visualization they try to transform the five impure gross skandhas into the five pure wisdom skandhas, the five Buddha families or deities. The essence of luminosity is clear space, so the deity and his clear space consort are always inseparable.

From the beginning, basic limitless luminosity mind is inherent within the limited path luminosity of the practitioner. If in this life our meditation practice is strong and continuous, then the luminosity of our dream phenomena and the luminosity of our waking phenomena are continuous in the same way as the sun sets while the full moon rises. When we separate from our present karmic body, our path luminosity is like a son recognizing his basic limitless luminosity mother and joining with her. If we have confidence at death, time habit is gone, place habit is gone, division habit is gone, and path habit is gone. Then there is no more path luminosity, only its result, which is pure, unobstructed, clear space luminosity, inseparable from basis luminosity.

According to the Great Perfection system, from the beginningless beginning our mind is pure, free, and luminous, so there is no division between the outer gross elements of the five skandhas and the inner subtle elements of the five skandas. The practitioner should only rest in the deep, fresh, all-pervasive self-secret purity, beyond obscured words and conceptions, of Wisdom Mind, which is stainless, clear luminosity space.

Usually, when we experience clear space in our meditation we grasp at it more and more. Then clear space disappears. If we see clear space beyond dullness when we meditate, we must not grasp at this clarity, thinking our meditation is very good. We must only relax and rest with this clear space mind so that the next time we meditate, we may join easily with clarity. If we stop our meditation in the midst of grasping turbulent thoughts, then, when we begin again, we reconnect with grasping and turbulence, and cannot relax. The most important practice is to relax in meditation without grasping. If gross elements conceptions arise, we must not chase after these conceptions in order to examine them.

If we are experienced meditators, when remembering mind recognizes gross element conceptions, we must just remain in mindfulness. According to a Mahasandhi text, if we chase after conceptions, more conceptions arise, producing more confusion and trouble, and we are like the stupid dog who chases after every stone instead of concentrating on the stone thrower. If we just remain in mindfulness, we are like the lion who kills the stone thrower instead of chasing after the stone.

As we become more experienced meditators, we are able to recognize our conceptions as they arise, just as we recognize an acquaintance on the street without needing to be introduced. Through this recognition, we can liberate our conceptions into clarity. If we continuously meditate, our remembering mind becomes more powerful than the beginning meditator's mind and does not have to depend on any special method or antidote to liberate our conceptions. It is like a snake whose knots effortlessly untie themselves, or it is like writing in water with your finger. As you are writing, the writing is dissolving.

If through our experience we are able to continuously meditate, all conceptions arise only as display. We have no conception that what arises is or is not a conception. We have no fear of losing anything. Everything is meditation without intention. Whatever conceptions arise, there is no more rejection or acceptance conception. There is no more expectation of benefit. It is like a thief who enters an empty house.

All Buddhist meditation can be contained within two categories: shamatha meditation and vipashyana meditation. According to the Hinayana system, first, through weariness of samsara, the meditator's mind becomes very peaceful. This is shamatha meditation, when the mind is never swayed by the passions, like a still ocean without stormy waves. From this calm mind, meditators can gradually see their egoless nature which is vipashyana meditation, in order to reach the arhat's stage, annihilating the enemy passions.

According to the Mahayana system, when meditators realize the insubstantiality of all phenomena, their egoless Wisdom Mind, automatically their mind becomes calm and peaceful; this is shamatha meditation. When they realize their mind is beyond the two extremes of existence and nonexistence, which is vipashyana meditation, they reach the Buddhahood stage of enlightenment.

According to the general outer Vajrayana system, when meditators accomplishing samadhi have one-pointed faith towards the object of the deity, their mind becomes very peaceful and calm, unable to be penetrated by ordinary passions. This is shamatha meditation. Gradually through this samadhi, their ordinary body, speech, and mind become transformed into deity's Wisdom Body, Speech, and Mind, which is vipashyana meditation.

According to the general inner Vajrayana system, in samsara all countless existent phenomena are contained within the five skandhas and all countless Buddhas are contained within the five Buddha families. Samsara's passions cannot penetrate the practitioner's mind when, through visualization, the five skandhas transform into the five Buddha families, which are the pure secret light essence of visible phenomena inseparable with the invisible qualities of the five wisdom consorts of great emptiness. This is samatha meditation. Gradually, when there is no differentiation between samsara's impure phenomena and nirvana's pure phenomena, this becomes vipashyana meditation, which is the directionless wheel of Wisdom Deity's phenomena.

According to the Mahayana system, resting in stainless great emptiness is called nyamshag, "remaining in equanimity meditation." Whenever we remain in equanimity, we should not desire to accumulate merit of any external form, because equanimity is the greatest accumulation. As Milarepa said, "When you are in Mahamudra meditation, if you are concerned about accumulating the merits of body and speech, your Wisdom Mind may disappear." Whenever the mind moves from this stainless great equanimity and rests in its glow where everything that arises appears as illusory display, it is called jethob, "after experiencing equanimity meditation."

The pure power of illusory element phenomena comes from stainless emptiness space. This sky space energy permeates the gross element energy of phenomena so that everything appears subtle, light, and illusory. The benefit of jethob is that whoever sees all phenomena as display does not cling to or reject illusory objects and in this way is accumulating merit. As Tilopa said to Naropa, "Until we realize that all phenomena are unborn, we must continuously turn the wheel of the accumulations of merit and wisdom."

To many inexperienced practitioners, nyamshag means resting in a sitting posture and jethob means moving from a sitting posture. Whoever stays in equanimity mind with dharmata mindfulness is practicing nyamshag meditation even though their body may move and their speech may sound. Whoever moves from equanimity mind into the afterglow of that experience with perception mindfulness is practicing jethob meditation even though their body is still and their speech is silent.

According to the inner Vajrayana system, resting in stainless great emptiness is also called nyamshag. Whenever the mind moves from this stainless great equanimity and rests in its glow where everything that arises appears as deity, when all form appears as deity's body, all sound as deity's mantra or voice, all thought as deity's stainless Wisdom Mind, it is called jethob.

The pure power of Wisdom Deity phenomena comes from unobstructed stainless wisdom luminosity. This luminous energy, which is the essence of the deity, permeates the subtle ordinary and illusory energy of the elements so that they appear as Wisdom Deity phenomena. The benefit is that all impure phenomena, including ordinary illusory phenomena, are purified into deity's phenomena without clinging or rejecting.

If we practice continuously, as the distinction between stainless equanimity sky mind and deity phenomena diminishes and they become more and more inseparable, we approach enlightenment where there is no nyamshag and no jethob, no inside and no outside, only the measureless sphere of one mandala. If we differentiate between shamatha and vipashyana meditation, or between nyamshag and jethob, there is a path and there are different stages, according to different faculties. But whoever seriously wants to reach enlightenment without elaborate conceptions does not need to worry about moving through different stages like climbing a staircase. These elaborate categories come from differentiating between relative truth and absolute truth. To the practitioner who can meditate naturally, there is no difference between the perceiver, the perceived, and the perception, between sitting meditation and moving meditation, or between relative truth and absolute truth. To the practitioner who can meditate naturally, there is no more between. Buddha Shakyamuni said, "The true truth is unborn but children cling with hoarse voices to the Four Truths. For those who enter into the essence of nirvana, there is not even the name of one truth. Then where are the Four Truths? Nowhere."

According to the point of view of the mind section of the Great Perfection, from the beginning, without discriminating between shamatha and vipashyana meditation, or between nyamshag and jethob, we establish the four great samayas, which are:

Nonexistent samaya: We cannot find samsara's negative qualities or nirvana's positive qualities anywhere because, from the beginning, mind does not exist substantially; it never existed, it does not exist now, it will never exist in the future. Even though white or black clouds appear, they do not exist, because space is always inherently empty.

Sole samaya: Our mind, which is always one, is the sole source of whatever impure phenomena of samsara appear or whatever pure phenomena of nirvana appear. Countless stars, planets, moons, and suns are reflected in one great ocean.

Free samaya: Samsara's phenomena cannot infect and nirvana's phenomena cannot benefit, because mind is free from all extremes and limits. In the sky there are no directions or sides.

Spontaneous samaya: Samsara's countless desirable qualities and nirvana's measureless desireless qualities always arise unobstructedly. This is the essence and display of natural Wisdom Deity's magic dance. Compared with countless ordinary precious jewels, mind is priceless because all phenomena increase spontaneously from mind.

Whoever can practice these four great samayas is already enlightened, even though their body, which is the result of their previous ripened karma, appears to be ordinary form. At the end of their life, many ordinary practitioners hope for an auspicious death, to be surrounded by family and disciples, crying, praying, and worshipping in holy style. But when sublime practitioners die, they do not care whether their corpse is put on a golden throne, adorned with a jeweled crown, and praised and worshipped, or whether it is thrown in the mud of a ruined graveyard and insulted.

As Longchenpa, "All-Knowing Great Vast Space Wisdom Teacher," said: "When the true practitioner dies, he is like a beggar in the street, alone with no hope and no one taking care, like an infant who does not even have conceptions about birth and death."

As Longchenpa taught, whoever practices continuously and purely through realization of the Great Perfection point of view is enlightened again to againless enlightenment. The practitioner who remains confidently in one profound space in vast equanimity beyond conceptions of realization or not-realization, beyond conceptions of liberation and not-liberation, may have this life's form, but it is temporary like the garuda's eggshell. The garuda's offspring already has the confidence and capacity to fly while within its shell, so that when its shell breaks, it can immediately fly in the sky. If we can realize the Great Perfection point of view in this life, we will understand that from the beginning the self-awareness perfection garuda resides within our karmic body. Then, when we leave our karmic body, our inner wisdom garuda flies in the Dharmakaya sky.

Afterword

Whenever we hear from teachers or read in texts that Wisdom Mind is beginningless, we think this means sometime before the beginning, far away from this present moment. We must recognize that if from the beginning our Wisdom Mind is beginningless, it has no beginning, no end, and no between, so it is continuous and always present. This basic original beginningless conception is connected with our path beginningless conception. If through the beginningless path of practice we can recognize the beginningless basis, then there is no more time, only one beginningless beginning now within our mind.

This book comes from the beginningless beginning. Since there is no beginning, there is no end. Now this book is ended into endless wisdom space in which all elements become one pure unending secret essence.

Books by Thinley Norbu from Shambhala Publications

A Brief Fantasy History of a Himalayan

In this autobiographical narrative, Thinley Norbu describes his early years in "Snowland" (Tibet) as one of seven children of the renowned Nyingma master Kyabje Dudjom Rinpoche. After touching on his youthful training and experiences, Rinpoche describes how he traveled and taught in many different nations and cities in the East and West. Shifting between poetic observations and earthy humor, he shares stories of worldly and spiritual events accompanied by incisive commentary and sublime prayers.

A Cascading Waterfall of Nectar

The open and natural words of Thinley Norbu Rinpoche, uncomplicated by scholarly elaboration, flow here in the tradition of the direct transmissions of Buddhas and Bodhisattvas of the past. Through commentary on the Preliminary Practices (Ngöndrö) prayer from the treasure text of the great master Tragtung Düdjom Lingpa, insights into many central practices emerge in order to deepen understanding of the foundations of Vajrayana Buddhism.

Magic Dance: The Display of the Self-Nature of the Five Wisdom Dakinis

This is a unique and powerful presentation of the teachings of Tibetan Buddhism on the five elements: earth, water, air, fire, and space. Through teachings, stories, and his distinctive use of language, Thinley Norbu Rinpoche relates how the energies of the elements manifest within our everyday world, in individual behavior and group traditions, relationships and solitude, medicine and art.

The Small Golden Key to the Treasure of the Various Essential Necessities of General and Extraordinary Buddhist Dharma

In *The Small Golden Key*, Thinley Norbu Rinpoche explains in simple, concise language the important ideas and practices of Buddhism, with special attention to the Vajrayana teachings of Tibetan Buddhism. He discusses the origins of Buddhism in India and its spread to Tibet; the important lineages of Tibetan Buddhism, with emphasis on the Nyingma school; the differences between the Hinayana, Mahayana, and Vajrayana teachings; the outstanding features of the Mahayana; and some of the special qualities and practices of the Vajrayana.

The Sole Panacea: A Brief Commentary on the Seven-Line Prayer *to Guru Rinpoche That Cures the Suffering of the Sickness of Karma and Defilement*

Of all the heartfelt devotional prayers used as a support for Dharma practice, the *Seven-Line Prayer* is the most essential, often repeated many thousands of times by practitioners, especially of the Nyingma and Dzogchen traditions of Tibetan Buddhism. Although the prayer is short and simple, its different levels of meaning make this commentary a welcome study aid for practitioners.

Welcoming Flowers from Across the Cleansed Threshold of Hope: An Answer to Pope John Paul II's Criticism of Buddhism

In *Welcoming Flowers*, Thinley Norbu Rinpoche presents a timely counterpoint to Pope John Paul II's depiction of the Buddhist tradition. Addressing many perceived errors and misrepresentations, Norbu separates fact from fiction, revealing the true face of Buddhism and providing an indispensable practitioner's perspective.

White Sail: Crossing the Waves of Ocean Mind to the Serene Continent of the Triple Gems

Buddhism teaches that enlightenment is our natural state; the problem is that we do not recognize this state, owing to the mind's confusion about its true nature. Thinley Norbu presents the Buddhist view in a way meant to clear up misconceptions and awaken the reader's innate wisdom.